I FOR AN EYE

Notion Press

Old No. 38, New No. 6

McNichols Road, Chetpet

Chennai - 600 031

First Published by Notion Press 2016

Copyright © Babu Rajendran 2016

All Rights Reserved.

ISBN 978-93-5206-915-6

This book has been published in good faith that the work of the author is original. All efforts have been taken to make the material error-free. However, the author and the publisher disclaim the responsibility.

No part of this book may be used, reproduced in any manner whatsoever without written permission from the author, except in the case of brief quotations embodied in critical articles and reviews.

Dedicated to

My

Parents, Parents-in-law,

All my Teachers,

And all my patients.

They made me what I am today

Contents

Foreword ix

Acknowledgments xi

Preface xiii

1. In the Beginning — 1
2. Getting into Medicine was Harder than I Thought—Even Fifty Years Ago — 6
3. Preclinical @ Manipal — 12
4. The Day of the Hippo — 19
5. All We Wanted was a Roof over Our Heads — 24
6. Clinical @ Mangalore — 29
7. Internship/Senior House Surgeon — 38
8. Postgraduation — 49
9. Fellowship at Melbourne — 63
10. Finally in Practice — 72
11. As the Wheel Turns—in Rotary — 90
12. And Some Work for the Societies — 102

13. Travels and Tribulations	106
14. Las Vegas	122
15. In Conclusion	126
16. Half a Day in an Eye Hospital	127
Epilogue	*135*

Foreword

I for an Eye is written by one who can stand tall and write candidly about our own Dr Babu Rajendran—'the man with a laser pen.'

During Madras All India Ophthalmological Conference 1989 (AIOC '89), I was new to the eye world. A person was prowling at the meet handing out instructions in his crisp voice on the preconference day, as if he alone owned every responsibility of the event. When I enquired, someone told me that he had performed the first laser and the electronic-medical presentation in India. On hearing that, I gained a pride for being a part of the field and my fear of joining the 'World of EYE' was gone.

We fondly remember his Presidential address in Jaipur at the AIOC '09 (All India Ophthalmological Conference 2009) and how the General body at the meeting was taken aback when he adjourned the meeting for lack of quorum, only to reconvene it after thirty minutes (an obvious legal point, which we had missed all those years). Mesmerized, the GB resolved the controversial yet the landmark change to allow members to vote electronically whether they attended AIOC or not. The AIOC Quiz where we all could participate with cellphones was his brainchild. I will put a stop here to the introduction or else it will be a book on the 'legend' Babu!

I had seconded his caring wife, Girija's request to write a book. Therefore, I have written this foreword hearing only the synopsis. That is Babu—'abrupt and decisive, yet the impact is so fully right.' I wait with you all to read the man with an 'Eye beyond Ophthalmology.'

Babu, you are among those rare human beings who should never become extinct. We need to preserve your health for the wealth of 'I for an Eye.'

Let us read on…

– Dr Debasish Bhattacharya
President, AIOS 2015–16
Founder Chairman,
Disha Eye Hospitals. W. B. India.

Acknowledgments

Giri, my wife of forty-four years, for all the love and care,

My daughter Priya,

My son Sushil and his family,

My two brothers, Balu and Jayan, and my sister Pushpa, and their families,

For standing by my side in good times and in bad times, in sickness and in health.

Thanks a million, I couldn't have made it without you.

Also to my friend the President of The All India Ophthalmological Society Dr Debashish,

For readily agreeing to write the foreword.

Preface

If you can dream it, you can make it happen.
— Walt Disney (1901–1966)

A Malayalee by descent, I was born in Andhra Pradesh, had my schooling in Ceylon (now Sri Lanka), and in the British Colony of North Borneo (now called Sabah and part of Malaysia); my medical education was in Karnataka, and I finally married and was domiciled in Tamil Nadu. Therefore, it is not strange that I can speak English, Malayalam, Kannada, Tamil, Sinhalese, and Malay fluently, and can even understand Tulu and Telugu. I can also read and write Latin, which I had to study in Colombo, as well as the second language that I learned at the pre-university, which I did in Kerala. As a ten-year-old boy in Colombo, I had my first contact with an ophthalmologist when I was taken for a checkup for a recurrent headache. The doctor was a family friend, and I was exposed to his eye clinic for the first time. The entire incident left a very deep impression on me; so, I too wanted to become an eye doctor. So, I carried this dream through my entire schooling, until I reached medical college. I spent about eleven years in Kasturba Medical College, Manipal and Mangalore, having finished MBBS and afterwards my MS there.

A senior Professor of General Surgery in Chennai told me on the day I started my clinic, "It does not matter what you were in Australia or Manipal. You are starting here from zero.

So be patient, regular, punctual, honest, and sincere in your work. It will take you seven years to establish yourself." And jokingly added, "If at the end of the seven years you haven't, then you are in the wrong place or the wrong profession." It did take me almost seven years from that day to realize and feel relaxed that I was in the right place and right profession. I charged Rs 25 as a consultation fee at a time when petrol was selling for Rs 28 a gallon (five liters). I used to run between three different hospitals in Chennai. I traveled once a month to Trichy at the invitation of Dr Rajasekar, traveled to Manipal once in two months to help them set a full-fledged retina service, and while returning, stopped for a couple of days at Dr Oommen's clinic in Cannanore to help him with his retinal cases. Those were very tiring and exhausting times.

I finally settled down at Vijaya Hospital in 1979; and in 1983, with the help of some well-wishers, I started The Eye Research Foundation, also located at Vijaya Hospital. We had the first Tunable Dye Laser, east of the Suez Canal, were one of the pioneers of Excimer Laser Refractive surgery, had the first computerized eye department, and developed the first automated angiography reporting system, among many other firsts; it was an exciting and fascinating journey.

"An Eye for an Eye
Will Make
The Whole World Blind"
– Mahatma Gandhi

"I have now spent the last four decades curing the blind," and *this is my story…*

The names of some people and places have been changed to protect the privacy of the individuals concerned.

In the Beginning

It was a cold dark night in Vizagapattinam, in South India. It had been raining for the past three days and nights. There was a cyclone brewing in the Bay of Bengal and the weather was most likely to get worse.

Thirty-five year old Hon Lt Dr Pillai, a member of the Royal Army Veterinary Corp., was pacing the corridors of the King George Hospital for the past couple of hours. His twenty-five-year-old wife Rajam had been wheeled into the labor room of the Maternity ward and they were all waiting for the Obstetrician, Dr Marikar, who had told them that if she did not deliver by that night, then she would have to do a caesarean section in the early morning the next day. The doctor was delayed, having been caught up in the rain and thunderstorm.

This was a precious baby to the Pillai's. They had been waiting nine years for this. The baby was already nine days overdue. They had had a very rough time for the last several years. Dr Pillai was posted with the Mounted Corps of the 17th Infantry Division in Burma during the World War II, at the end of 1941 and early 1942, when it was evident that the Japanese army was headed towards Rangoon, in particular, and Burma, in general. Soon, the families were ordered to evacuate at short notice from Rangoon by the last ship leaving for India. With no other alternative, Rajam and her widow mother (Chellamma) had boarded the ship and returned to India and eventually to their native place in South India,

Trivandrum. Dr Pillai hailed from a nearby town called Punalur, at the foothills of the Eastern Ghats.

The bridge across the Sittang River had been blown up to prevent the Japanese advance, but unfortunately, many men of the 17th Division were still on the Eastern side. In enemy territory, Dr Pillai was one among them. He got separated from the large column of retreating soldiers due to Japanese ambush locations and escaped by avoiding the main roads in order not to get detected. They also traveled only at night.

At the height of the war and the famous retreat by troops from Burma, he, alongside a few of his colleagues, trekked over the course of many days and nights back to Calcutta. The retreating soldiers, after their hundred-mile ordeal, were described by General Slim as "utterly exhausted, riddled with malaria and dysentery."[1] Dr Pillai and his two friends reached Calcutta many weeks later looking even worse than what General Slim had said. He took another two weeks to reach his home in Trivandrum and more than eighteen months to recuperate, having already got an honorable discharge from the army on medical grounds.

When he did recover, he joined the government service and was posted in Vizagapattinam, which was why he was here pacing the hospital corridor.

The pains had started in the afternoon during lunch, and, with great difficulty, Rajam was brought to the hospital. A messenger had informed Dr Marikkar. The call to the doctor and the membrane rupture occurred at the same time, around 7 pm. There was no word from the labor room. Suddenly, the door opened at about 8 pm and the gynecologist came out and informed that the baby was too big and that she had decided to go ahead with the C-section. Rajam was shifted to the trolley for transfer to the operating room. As soon as the transfer was done, the pains increased, as the baby was

---

1 www. historylearningsite. co. UK

beginning to come out. They never made it to the OT. On that rainy night, with the winds lashing at the windows and the trees swaying, as if about to break, lying on that trolley, the baby was delivered. At 9:10 pm, he took his first breath in the world, gave a mighty scream, and announced his arrival. The heavily built Anglo-Indian Matron (more Anglo than Indian) announced the baby's arrival to the proud dad. "It's a boy! A BIG BOY!" Tipping the scales at just over 10.25 lbs (3.8 Kg), the author had arrived, five months and five days after World War II had ended.

Soon after that, my dad left his job in Vizag and went off to Ceylon (Now Sri Lanka) to join the government service there. His first posting was in the town of Batticaloa on the Eastern seaboard. My maternal grandmother was also with us. We were there for a little over three years. In fact, my brother was born there in 1948, and again we moved, this time with my father, who got promoted to the bigger Veterinary hospital close to Kandy, a rather big town. My second brother was born there two years later, and our only sister another two years after that.

The next was a major and significant jump to Colombo, where my dad took over the job of Veterinary Superintendent at the Dehiwala Zoo, which at the time was considered to be one of the top ten zoos in the world. We spent the majority of our childhood there. Our house was within the zoo compound; so as kids, we had a rollicking time there, handling majority of the animals, from large cats, tigers, lions, leopards, apes like chimpanzees, and orangutans, to the more docile deer and birds of all types. We were the source of envy for all our classmates and relatives. I specifically remember a large chimp called Steven who was in a cage close to our house. Every evening, this ape would sit at a table with a cigarette, which he smoked stylishly. My dad had a habit of giving him a sweet every night on his way back home, and on the rare occasion that he forgot, my dad was promptly reminded by the screeches and banging on the door of the cage till he was given that sweet.

We played with very young baby elephants, one in particular called "*Bandulla,*" which probably was only a few weeks old at that time. We rode ponies, horses, elephants, and camels to our hearts' content. The worst and troubling thing in those years was the fact that our mother fell ill. She was diagnosed with a heart condition called atrial septal defect (ASD), which in those days could be a life-threatening ailment. She was well taken care of though, and went about her normal activities. Unfortunately, she got the Asian flu epidemic in 1957, which resulted in developing pericarditis and her heart decompensated. She rapidly declined in health only to pass away in May 1958. Our grandmother brought us up after that.

Around that time, an uprising began in Ceylon between the Sinhalese and the Tamils and many of the Indians were returning to India. In 1961, our family too returned to Trivandrum enrooted to the British Colony of North Borneo (now the State of Sabah, part of Malaysia). I had finished my Cambridge "O" level and left before doing the "A" level. That I did in Jesselton, the capital of Borneo (now called Kota Kinabalu).

Our contact and fondness did not leave us here. My dad was posted to be in charge of the largest Veterinary station there and we had our house within that compound. Very often, many young orangutan babies found abandoned in the jungles of Borneo were brought here to be looked after until they were big enough to be rehabilitated, before being let into the wild again. It was our daily chore to feed those babies from feeding bottles every evening, a task all of us siblings thoroughly enjoyed. At one time, there were as many as eleven baby apes we were looking after.

We went to a school in Jesselton with many teachers from Ceylon and South India. Dr Radcliffe, our headmaster, was a very tough disciplinarian, and taught us English and Scottish dancing! I passed my "A" level and had no option but to go back to India for higher education.

However, I had about six months until that happened, and took up my first job as a broadcasting technician in Radio North Borneo broadcasting from Jesselton. While the station started its broadcast at 6 am with a recorded version of the day's news from Radio Australia, my job entailed opening up the station at 5 am, and switching on all recorders and transmitters. Specifically, I needed to transmit a 2 KHz signal by 5:30 am to activate a transmitter on top of Mount Kinabalu (the highest mountain in that region). By getting that signal, the transmitter was switched on and responded with a 1 KHz signal, which we picked up and knew all was well. In between that, I had to record the morning news relayed from Radio Australia and keep it cued for broadcast. It was a fun job that I thoroughly enjoyed, and learned a great deal about recording, broadcasting, announcing, etc. In April of 1964, I landed in Madras in South India hoping to join a medical college.

Getting into Medicine was Harder than I Thought—Even Fifty Years Ago

So I carried this dream during my schooling days. I finished Cambridge "O" level in Colombo when we moved to Borneo, and finished my Cambridge "A" Level with four A's. This was an extremely difficult exam of a very high standard.

I then got the address of all the medical colleges in India, from the Indian High Commission in Singapore, and applied to all seventy-two (I think) colleges that were there at that time. Since I was applying from Malaysia, most colleges asked me to either apply to the Ministry of Foreign affairs or through the High Commission or asked me to come and meet them personally, except the Lady Harding Medical College, Delhi, who wrote: *"Madam this college is only for women."* It was while waiting for the replies that I took up the job in Radio Malaysia Sabah, as a broadcasting technician. It was a challenging task that exposed me to strict discipline and taught me the importance of punctuality (a trait, most people know, I carry even today), since every action in the studio was clocked to the last second.

It was only later when I was informed that I could not get into any medical college in India, since the 'A' level was not a recognized qualification at that time for medical entrance. Some teacher friends of the family suggested I return to India and repeat a pre-university. One day, before the Onam holidays (and the end of the first term), I enrolled for the pre-university course at a college in Ernakulum. I was totally lost in the unknown environment. All my A-level subjects were of no use. I had to study English, English literature, Mathematics, Science, Indian History, World History, Social Studies, and a second language!! Indian History and the second language were giving me nightmares and I was sure that my medical dreams were about to go out of the window. I had panic attacks that I had no option but to return to Malaysia to my broadcasting job (which I had actually begun to enjoy). In order to avoid having to return to Malaysia, in a moment of desperation, I applied to the Indian Air Force to be a pilot (but the application was rejected outright since I was too tall!!), and to the Film Institute at Poona to be a cinematographer (but got no reply from them). Had I been selected, this article may be appearing in the *Filmfare* magazine and would probably be titled an '*EYE for an I*'!!

The principal of the college had sent his peon to pay my fees before twelve noon, and asked his secretary to take me to whichever period was going on then, so that I would get attendance from the morning session onwards. I was taken to a room where a Chemistry class was going on. The lecturer was quite annoyed at being disturbed and more so by my late admission. He gave me a talk on about how much I had already missed much and that he could not repeat all of that. I told him that I would manage, wondering what indeed I had missed. I had just done "A" level Chemistry, inorganic, some organic, and Physical Chemistry, analyzed double salts for the exam, and to my delight and dismay, this class was about copper sulphate. He was saying, "Copper Sulphate is Blue," and then repeated the whole thing in Malayalam. This was the same with the math class and the other Science subjects. I hit the roadblock in Indian History. I was seeing such unpronounceable names for the first time. Eventually, I just learned them by heart.

When I first joined the college, I was staying with my father's elder brother who lived in a small town, some thirty-five miles (57 kms) away. I used to travel up and down daily, traveling for about two hours each way by bus. The very first day, I arrived at the bus stop headed towards Ernakulum, I noticed a private bus just pulling out of the stop. I enquired from someone standing there in Malayalam, the vernacular language of the state, how I could get to Ernakulum; he replied in Malayalam, something to the effect that Parvathi (a woman's name) would come in ten minutes and would just leave quickly, since she will be going very fast. I was flabbergasted and then wondered whether Parvathi was driving a car. But, I got more confused when he continued and said that Vasanthi and Kamala would follow. By the time I got over the shock of this, Parvathi did arrive, a brand new luxurious looking private bus, and only then did I realize that most buses and trucks bore feminine names prominently written across the front, above the windscreen. I traveled thus for a couple of months and then I found that it took more and more time for the trip, due to road and bridge repairs along the way. So, my uncle found me an accommodation with another relative who had just returned from overseas, and lived with his family at a place close to the college. They were a highly lovable and loving family of four (one son being away in the armed forces). They converted a garage into a modified room and I stayed there. That uncle was allergic to cow's milk, I believe, and so they kept a goat at home. As part of my efforts to help in the household chores, I used to milk the goat every morning. That was the time that India was going through the period after the Indo-China war of 1962, and everything was in short supply. Sugar and rice were very difficult to get and we had to use palm jaggery instead as the sweetener. Even now, the thought of coffee early morning with goat's milk and *pal* jaggery makes me wonder why I just never had black coffee instead. I had now plenty of time to read, saving nearly four to five hours of traveling. This uncle had a Vauxhall Velox car, which he had brought back along with him, and every morning I drove him to his office after dropping off his son and daughter in school, and then walked to my college, which was just two blocks away. In the evenings, this process was reversed. All in all, this was a very comfortable period of my life.

The pre-university exams were fast approaching and my mugging of History reached a feverish pitch. Actually, that was all I studied and a bit of the second language. On the day before the first exam, English I (or whatever), at about 7 pm, there was a big commotion outside my room. When I went outside and looked, the entire family was standing and peering into the well at the back of their house. I joined the others and found the neighbor's dog had fallen in and was struggling to stay afloat. We tried lowering the bucket, but the dog showed no signs of wanting to get into it or even holding on to it. Finally, I had to get into the well and put the dog into the larger bucket that was lowered, and so the dog was rescued. But, the matter didn't end there. Some helpful or rather over helpful neighbors said the entire well had to be emptied and bleaching powder added before we could use it again. So, I spent almost the rest of the night emptying the well (luckily it was a very shallow well with not too much water, while my uncle went looking for bleaching powder). And so, I went to the English exam, half sleepy, really tired, and probably smelling of bleaching powder as well.

It was in this college that I had a group of friends some of who were rather weak (to say the least) in English and I often helped them with their English assignments. In the English question paper, we had one question based on the non-detailed textbook. This book usually contained the life histories of some famous people like Alfred Noble, Louis

Braille, Louis Pasteur, etc. One day, this group of friends came to me and said they had analyzed past papers and had come to the conclusion that this year there was a strong possibility the question would be on Braille. So, they wanted me to write an essay on Braille, which they would study. I said I would, but forgot about it since there were a couple of months left to the exam. But, a week later, to the day, they cornered me and wanted the essay. I promised to give it to them the next day and that night wrote an essay about Louis Braille based on the material in the book. Photocopying machines were not so common those days, so these guys copied the essay so that each person had his own copy. I of course soon forgot the exact wording in the essay that I had written. A few days later, they told me that they were ready. "For what?" I asked. "To tell you the essay on Braille." "What?" I asked. And they explained to me that whatever they studied they kept repeating among themselves so that they were thorough. I found that a fascinating idea. So from then on, whenever we were walking to or from the college, one of them would repeat the entire passage *verbatim*. In fact, they would say things like, he was born in France comma in a small town near Paris dot, and God forbid if there was a semicolon in the sentence, they would say dot and a comma (they never said full stop! Little realizing that the same full stop would to be called a dot many decades later in the Internet era, e.g., gmail. com, very much like people referring to the @ symbol in an email id as "at the rate of," since that was what it was called earlier!!). In any case, within a few weeks, they were all thorough with the entire essay in which I had started saying—"In the year 1809, Louis Braille was born in a small town near Paris...."

Sure enough, when the exam came, the non-detail question was on Louis Braille. I looked at my friends and they were all giving each other the thumbs-up sign. After the exam, I had demanded that they buy me a coffee and they agreed, except one of them who looked dejected. When asked why he was so, he replied that he could not write the Braille question since he had forgotten the start of the sentence, "In the year 1809!!"

Eventually, the results came, and I had passed with a distinction; in fact, I had even scored more marks in the second language than in English (probably because of the dog in the well, or so I consoled myself).

A fresh round of applications to medical colleges, but this time, I applied only to the Trivandrum Medical College and CMC Vellore, and went with a cousin of mine and his father to personally apply and attend an entrance examination in Manipal. When we arrived there, it was raining, and boy was it raining. It rained heavily nonstop for every single minute of the two days we were there. The founder, Dr T.M.A. Pai addressed an auditorium packed with over two thousand new applicants (for 200 seats), and said, "*if you do not get selected this year, come back again next year and then the year after that and we will definitely give you a seat then.*" "Forget it," I said to myself, "Come back to this rain-soaked place—Never." But my dream of being an eye doctor kept flashing before me. The guided tour they gave us through the very famous anatomy museum gave my cousin and me the adrenaline rush we needed.

Eventually, I spent close to eleven years in Manipal/Mangalore, having finished MBBS and then my MS there. So much so that even today I miss that wonderful rain. On every available opportunity, I rush back to Manipal, which became my second home.

Preclinical @ Manipal

Both my cousin Ravi and I did very well and were selected, and we joined premedical, having paid a capitation fee of a princely sum of 5000 rupees.

The first year in medical college at that time was called the premedical or the pre-professional course and was actually the second year of the pre-university course; we had to study Physics and Chemistry, Zoology, Botany, English, and a little bit of Statistics. There was no second language and finally no World or Indian History. These subjects, other than the Statistics, were still far less a standard than the **A** level that I had already done. It was therefore a fun year for me, and even the thought of an exam at the end of it did not seem to frighten me.

About two months after we joined Manipal and when the rains had stopped, one day while peeping through the window of the hostel room, I noticed a few people playing cricket on a practice pitch in the corner of the football field. Immediately, I put on my canvas shoes and ran to the ground. I had been playing cricket since my school days and actually had played at the college level as well. There were only a handful of people playing cricket that day, and as I went, stood and watched, one of them asked me if I wanted to bat. They were playing on a matting on the practice pitch and people were taking turns to bat. I told that I would rather bowl, since inherently I was a bowler and a very bad batsman. The next over, the ball was thrown to me, and I had the opportunity to bowl the first ball in this college. I had no idea who was batting, but whoever it was, I managed to get him bowled in the next three constitutive balls. At the end of the over, somebody sitting at the side of that practice pitch called me, and when I went, he introduced himself as the Physical Director and wanted to know how long I had been playing cricket. He said the college badly needed an opening bowler and wanted me to come for practice every day thereafter. I did attend these practice sessions and was selected to the college team as the opening bowler, a position I held for many years.

Cricket aside, studies went on in full swing. There was also a compulsory National Cadet Corp. (NCC) for all the boys in the class, the girls having been exempted from this. Our Botany lecturer, Mr Bairy, was the Second Lieutenant in charge of this activity, and Subedhar Major Kunjuraman was (I think that was his name) the person deputed by the army to conduct these exercises.

Is it was at this time that my father and grandmother came to Manipal to pay me a visit before they returned to Malaysia. My father being an ex-army man, he wanted to watch our NCC training. Unfortunately for me, the day he came, two of my friends in the NCC Battalion got up to some mischief, and the commanding NCC officer had made us run around the football ground for the entire duration of that training and that was about all my father got to see. NCC itself was great fun, and apart from repeated training in marching and other activities, we had rifle training and were also taken out to camps. Because of my height, I was always the right marker in the platoon, and at the camp, I was made the ADC to the Camp Commandant. This meant that I did not have to go on the long route marches that the rest of the Battalion made on and off throughout the ten days we were there. Eventually, I was elected the best cadet for that year, which made my father very proud indeed. The exams came at the end of the year, which was actually a cakewalk for me, and it and I ended up doing very well, with me being one of the toppers in that class. After the annual holidays, we returned to join the first year of MBBS of preclinical training at Manipal.

This was when we actually thought we had become doctors. White coats were compulsory and we carried dissection instruments in our pockets and spent the whole morning in the anatomy hall dissecting dead bodies. The first day in the dissecting hall saw everybody tearing away till the end of the session, as the hall was full of formalin, since the room was surrounded by formalin and the bodies for dissection were pulled out of the formalin-filled storage tanks and laid out on steel-topped tables for us to dissect. There were four to eight of us at each table, and we had a whole body to ourselves; while somebody dissected the palm, another group started with the dissection of the feet on each side, and then we worked ourselves towards the center of the body. Some people developed an allergy to the formalin and were forced to wear gloves; the others were not allowed to wear gloves. Anatomy involved the dissections, theory classes, and practicals in histology (or Microscopic anatomy). Anatomy as a subject did not seem, to me, as something that could be understood or learned with logic. It looked like it had to be memorized like multiplication tables. Physiology on the other hand was of great interest to me, and if we understood the principles and logic, then we did not have to by heart anything. We also had to do Biochemistry, for which we had a very tough lecturer who on the very first day lay down the rules that were to be followed in his class. Eventually, he became a great friend of ours, though in the class he was as strict as ever. Biochemistry was tough, physiology was interesting and therefore easy, and anatomy was ridiculously hard to study; the very look of the fat Greys anatomy and the three volumes of Cunningham sent shudders through me, wondering how on earth I was going to remember all that stuff. It was during the first year of this one and a half year first MBBS that I was elected the President of the Students' Association, which was being revived after being having been defunct for some time. Since I had done very well in the premedical course, by the time I came to this first MBBS part, all the lecturers, professors, and other staff knew the top ten students in the class, and we always got caught for all discussions in the class. This actually turned out to be an advantage since it forced us to be well prepared before we entered the class itself, and therefore maybe even to understand class better. Anatomy also required the maintenance of a record book with drawings of the parts that we dissected. Unluckily for me, like many others in my batch, we had no sense of drawing. About four months into the course, we came to know from our seniors that there were some chaps working in the anatomy museum who were excellent artists and were willing to draw our record books according to our specifications for payment of a small fee. This obviously was the way we thought to go about this rather than wasting a lot of time trying to do it ourselves, which I could use more usefully in studying. About six months into the first MBBS, we were taught clinical physiology, and after being taught how to do blood counts, et cetera, we were taught how to take the blood pressure. The college Dean, who was also the Professor of Physiology, broke the group into batches of three, and each was supposed to record the BP of the other two in the group. Ravi and Bhupi were the other two in my group; first Ravi took my BP and got a reading of 160/100. Both looked at me and I laughed thinking that he had not taken the reading properly. Bhupi then tried and got the same reading, while we were discussing this and thought probably the instrument was faulty. So, I recorded the BP for the other two, which came as expected, 120/80. We were having a big discussion about my reading when the Dean, who was the Professor of Physiology, came in angrily and asked us what we were discussing rather than doing what we were supposed to. They told him that my BP was being recorded very high and he recorded it himself and got the same high reading. I was only in my early twenty's then, and so the Dean sent me to see the physician in the OPD. He had rung up and informed that I would be coming to the OPD. The physician examined me with his registrar and got the same high reading and said it might be because I had walked from the Physiology lab all the way to the hospital, and so, he asked me to lie down for some time on the bed and told the registrar to check my BP after half an hour; when this did not come down, together they examined me in detail. The registrar kept saying something like "there is a bruit, sir," and the physician came and checked me and said that he could not hear it. This all sounded Greek and Latin to me at that time, but subsequently I was asked to go back, and the physician said that at some stage I needed to get a renal angiogram done. Since it was not available at that time in Manipal, I was told I could get it done at CMC, available if I ever went that way.

Nothing was done about this since many others thought that this was an inherited form of essential hypertension and I did nothing till I was forty years when another physician in Chennai said that it was time to start treating it (I now realize that at that time it was indeed essential hypertensions, because now all my siblings, both my children, and some of their cousins also have hypertension and are being treated for it.)

For some unknown reason from my initial MBBS days, I had an aversion to studying about the kidney. I had problems with the anatomy, physiology, and even the embryology and histology of the kidney. This is something I carried on through the entire course of my medical studies, having an aversion to its Pathology, medicine, and surgery of kidney diseases.

In the first MBBS, in the mornings, we came back from the anatomy lab smelling of formalin and dead tissue, and many of my friends have landed up sitting for lunch only to find a piece of flesh from the dissection, stuck to their fingers! In the afternoon, we came back with the hands covered in soot or the black from the smoked drum that was used in the frog experiments. These were frogs (rather large in size, specially bred by the college for these classes) that were pithed, meaning paralyzed rather than dead, so that we could detect neuromuscular reactions and cardiovascular changes to different stimuli. Very often one of these frogs would sit up on the table and many of my female classmates have screamed and run out of the class or fainted in the class itself. The eighteen months of the first MBBS went by very quickly and soon the time came for the exam. This was the first time that we were being exposed to four examiners for each subject, three external and one internal. This went on throughout the medical career in each of the subjects that had examination. I once calculated that by the time I went through medical college, I had passed through the hands of over fifty examiners, other than those who corrected the theory papers.

In anatomy, we had a histology exam, a dissection, and a viva. I got to dissect the testicular artery. The examiner seemed to be a nasty old man who I heard screaming at the frightened students at each table that he went to. When he came to my table, he asked me what I had been asked to dissect, and when I said the testicular artery, he asked to show it to him, and I did show it from end to end because I had done a very good dissection. Suddenly, he asked me to show the testicular artery on the other side, which I was not required to dissect. I picked up what I thought was that testicular artery and the examiner picked up something similar with a hook and looked at me and in a loud voice said, "Now this man has three testicular arteries. How many do you have?" he asked, and left me with that. In the afternoon, I bumped into him again for the osteology viva (study of the bones); again, he was rather nasty but I got through the viva and the exam as well. The rest of the exams in the subjects went off well and I did pass the first MBBS, once again at the top of the class. At this stage in those days, we had to go to Mangalore of to do the rest of our MBBS, the clinical course as it was called, since the college was attached to the government Wenlock Hospital ere. Shifting from quiet Manipal to a busier Mangalore was an experience in itself. Getting the proper hostel accommodation was also quite a challenge, since the previous batch had not yet vacated.

The Day of the Hippo

I can't believe that nearly fifty years have passed since I left KMC Manipal. Those were the days when just joining a medical college made us feel that we were already halfway to becoming doctors. Just wearing the white coat to anatomy dissection, or the frog dissection in physiology, felt like doing brain surgery. Those were the days when we lived a whole month on 200 rupees (including the mess bill!).

Manipal was not more than a hillock back then. Leopards and hyenas roamed around. Just walking back from after a night show required walking in large groups as means of safety.

Life at the undergraduate level was full of fun and frolic (except for the exams—yuck!). I can recall several memorable things about those days, like winning the first election as President of the Students' Association, but undoubtedly, the thing that really stands out the most is the prank we played on one of the members of our staff.

Bupinder Patel (formerly from Lusaka, Zambia, now in the USA), my cousin the late Ravindran Pillai (formerly from Sri Lanka, then in Hawaii), and I (formerly from Malaysia, now in Chennai) were all members of the college cricket team.

Bhupi was a great opening batsman, Ravi was our wicket keeper cum the other opening batsman, and I was the opening bowler. We were all staying in the same room, in the main block (now the women's hostel). Our Physical Director (PD), Mr Shetty, was an extremely nice and likeable person. However, he had this bad habit of getting angry if we played badly. As a form of punishment, he would force us back to the hostel for lunch instead of giving us lunch at a hotel in Udupi as was planned. After all, in those days, one of the charms of playing cricket for the college was that we got to go to such beautiful places, such as Mangalore, Mysore, Bangalore, and others with the team. More importantly, we could go and have a nice Sunday lunch in a hotel in Udupi after the game.

Anyway, in the first MBBS vacation, we were all going away to our respective homes. We asked the PD what he wanted us to get him from our trip.

The poor man was not even aware of what each country was famous. Then I said that Malaysia had good Batik shirts, so he told me to get him one. Ravi talked about the famous Sri Lankan tea, and he said that he would like to have that. He asked Bhupi what Zambia was famous for, and we all said, "Hippos." Well, PD said, "Get me one then!"

Off we went on our vacations and the matter was forgotten for the time being. When we returned, I gave him the Batik shirt and Ravi gave him the tea he had requested. Bupi gave him a shirt too, I think, but the PD wanted to know what had happened to the Hippo he asked for. Bupi just replied, "It's coming," and left it at that.

A couple of weeks later, it was a bad weekend, and all three of us had done miserably in the match against MGM. Both Bhupi and Ravi got out without scoring, and Ravi dropped two catches and missed a stumping. To make matters worse, I was hit all around the park for fours and sixes by a guy who went on to became the university opener. I think he even went to play in Ranji Trophy (an Interstate Cricket Tournament in India). Off course, after the match, we were promptly sent back to the mess for lunch.

We were quite upset because only two weeks before that we had given the PD all those gifts. Yet here we were now, missing out on a biryani lunch on a nice Sunday afternoon.

That's when we realized something and made a plan—***THE HIPPO***.

On Monday evening, we went off to Udupi and got hold of some dirty brownish paper—like the ones in which the government letters are typed on. Then, we went to a typist near Udupi court and had a letter typed out and addressed to the PD. I don't recall the exact content, but it was something along these lines,

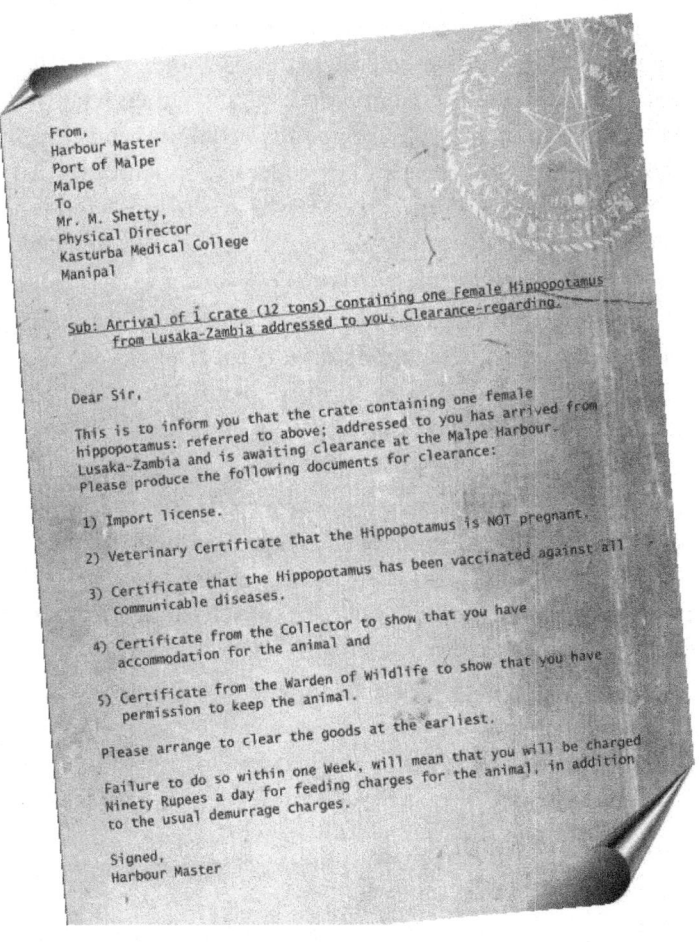

From,
Harbour Master
Port of Malpe
Malpe

To
Mr. M. Shetty,
Physical Director
Kasturba Medical College
Manipal

Sub: Arrival of 1 crate (12 tons) containing one Female Hippopotamus from Lusaka-Zambia addressed to you. Clearance-regarding.

Dear Sir,

This is to inform you that the crate containing one female hippopotamus; referred to above; addressed to you has arrived from Lusaka-Zambia and is awaiting clearance at the Malpe Harbour. Please produce the following documents for clearance:

1) Import license.

2) Veterinary Certificate that the Hippopotamus is NOT pregnant.

3) Certificate that the Hippopotamus has been vaccinated against all communicable diseases.

4) Certificate from the Collector to show that you have accommodation for the animal and

5) Certificate from the Warden of Wildlife to show that you have permission to keep the animal.

Please arrange to clear the goods at the earliest.

Failure to do so within one Week, will mean that you will be charged Ninety Rupees a day for feeding charges for the animal, in addition to the usual demurrage charges.

Signed,
Harbour Master

We placed the very authentic-looking letter in a government-looking envelope and sent it to him. Two days went by while we were waiting for the letter to be delivered. On the third day, while we were in the physiology lecture class being taught by Dr Krishna Rao, our Dean, the PD was at the door wanting to speak to Bhupi. And then, the fun began! Bupi went out and spoke to him and then came back and got permission for Ravi and I to also leave the class.

The PD looked like he was about to have a number of epileptic fits. He was telling Bupi that he really didn't want the Hippo and that he only meant it as a joke, while Bupi kept saying that he had mentioned it to his father who then readily arranged one to be shipped. He couldn't send it back now. "It would cost thousands of rupees in freight," we told him. What was he going to do with it? Where would he keep it? How was he to get the pregnancy certificate? Ninety rupees a day! *A hippopotamus in Manipal?*

These were all the questions that must have been going through his mind. He wanted answers for all of this while we were seated in a Shangri-La restaurant. He was buying us coffee and dosas in an effort to try and get our help.

Finally, he decided he would go and ask Mr Ramesh Pai what to do because Bupi had suggested the Hippo could be kept in the Manipal Lake. While waiting in the Academy Office to see Mr Ramesh Pai, who was fortunately busy, we noticed the poor man was trembling and then he started sweating and that's when we told him the truth.

It would be ungentlemanly for me to write what was said or what happened shortly after that, but we were suspended from the team for the next three matches. Fortunately, later he saw the funny side of it and we were all became friends again.

Yes, those were the days...

Seated L to R: PD Mudonna Shetty, and Me
Standing 1" w R to L: Bhupi
Standing - rcw R to L: 3" Ravi

CRICKET TEAM

HOWZAT ? UNIVERSITY CHAMPS !

All We Wanted was a Roof over Our Heads

After two and half years in Manipal, I was looking forward to going to Mangalore, to join the clinical side, with great expectation.

Six of us, Bhaskar, Ramani, Umashankar, Kannan, Viji, and I (my friends in college called me Bobby) had ganged up already at Manipal and wanted to stay together at the Kaprigudda Hostel. When we landed in Mangalore, to our dismay, we found that there was no place at the Kaprigudda Hostel and we had to look for a place to stay outside.

The six Musketeers went around Mangalore mainly in and around Kaprigudda looking for a place to stay. We were chased away by the barking pet dogs in a few houses. In another few houses, the house owner virtually chased us away, probably to protect their daughters, but we continued in our search for a place and by evening found a place nearby. We decided that Bhaskar would do the talking, as we thought he was a charmer with landlords, especially the landladies. He went in and met the owner; she agreed to give us an accommodation, but said only four could stay in her house. Out of necessity, they had got a lovely house with mosaic flooring and all.

Viji and I volunteered to look for some other place. Night was fast approaching and we needed a place to sleep that night, and we were desperate. To our relief, we found a place nearby, a small and dingy place. It probably measured about ten feet by six feet (probably much smaller than a toilet in our present houses). It had a very low doorway and I had to hunch to enter. There was one tiny window about two feet square with some bars across. The room had two wobbly benches and one light (probably a zero watt bulb). This didn't bother us as we had a table lamp each; at that time we didn't realize that we didn't have a table nor was there a place to keep it in the room!! We just wanted a room over our heads.

The rent was ridiculously low; I haven't the vaguest idea how much it was but probably 120 rupees a month or so. The landlady was an elderly woman who told us in a very stern voice that we couldn't bring visitors to the room, make loud noises in the room, or use the radio after 10 pm. She showed us the toilet at the back of the house and the well nearby where we had to bathe. She said we were not to waste water and that if we dropped the bucket in the water, we had to get it out, pay someone to get it out, or buy a new bucket and rope. She said the light had to be switched off when we were not in the room and so many other conditions. Both of us nodded our heads like goats to everything she said, just showing how desperate we were. Anyway, she gave us a key and we paid a month's advance, which she emphasized was *'Not returnable.'*

She also mentioned how it was a lucky room and the previous tenant had passed and become a doctor, which is why he had left. Then just as we were going towards the room in a much sterner voice she said, "And Doctors! *No* talking to my daughter," "Yes Madam," the two goats nodded!! In our mind though we thought, "WOW! She has a daughter?"

As Viji and I were hungry as hell by then, we left our suitcases and bedrolls inside, went out and got something to eat. By the time we got back, having stopped to talk to many classmates also roaming around this new town, it was way past nine pm and we were dead tired and ready to lie down and doze off, or so we thought.

In the dim light of the room, we could hardly see the lock on the suitcases or the knot on the bedroll to undo it. Luckily, there was bright moonlight so we dragged all the stuff out and got out the stuff we needed and then took all the boxes and bedrolls back and got ready to sleep. We left the window open to allow some moonlight and some breeze to come in. Only then did we realize "*Houston we have a problem!*" as the saying goes. The wobbly bench was too narrow and too short for me. So, I offered to lie on the floor and he joined the two benches and put my bed roll over it. I think I was asleep before I hit the pillow.

Suddenly, Viji woke me up, "Bobby, Bobby get up," he said "There is someone outside the window." As I listened, sure enough there was a feeble voice "Doctor, Doctor," it said. We thought, dear God the old woman must be sick or something and the daughter is calling us. I kept whispering in Tamil, "ignore her," but he said what if it is a medical emergency and I asked if it is as if we know what to do what if she was dead!! Then what?

The voice grew closer and slightly louder, "Doctor, please answer me." Viji stood up, since it was easier for him to get up from the benches than for me to get up from the floor.

He went to the window and asked what she wanted and she said, "What time do you want to have bath in the morning?" "Six o'clock," he said

We should have guessed it then, which normal human being would wake up somebody close to 11 pm and ask what time we were going to bathe in the morning. We didn't! Dumb goats that we were, "*We needed a roof over our heads.*" We had a quick chat about it, is she nuts or what? But then decided, the innocent souls that we were, probably she had to keep hot water ready for the tenants. What a hope!

Anyway, all this meant we had to close the only window before we are disturbed again and tried to sleep. 'Tried' is the operative word here. The room was like a furnace, there was no air coming in or going out? The little physiology that we remembered after the exam we had passed came to mind. What was increased carbon dioxide levels called? Hypercapneia. That's it! Was there some carbon monoxide as well? Would we both be dead by morning?

We opened the door and sat at the doorway when sleep forced us back into the furnace. I was the happiest person to see sunlight peeping through. I jumped up and said I would go to the toilet and have a bath first because I had decided that I would go back to Manipal early morning to meet my brother at MIT (Manipal Engineering College, those days) and borrow the table fan he had in his room.

Viji was all game since that meant we wouldn't be roasted for a second night.

Off I went and Viji was trying to get his suitcase organized and then he was on his way to the toilet at the back of the house. Lo and behold, he got to see a sight for sore eyes, which he remembers even to this day.

There was this tall and lanky Bobby standing almost naked trying to have a bath from the well but also trying to cover oneself behind the rim of the well and the pillars.

And the reason? The landlady's twenty something daughter was seated a few feet away on a ledge ogling at naked me!!! Oh boy, was I glad to see him. He threw me his towel and got things sorted out. So, this was the daughter we were 'Not supposed to talk to.'

And all we wanted was a roof over our heads!! No to be a sideshow by the well.

That evening we went back to Kaprigudda Hostel, begged and pleaded, and were given a room. The famous Room No. three that was shared by Viji, Ramani, and me, where we had the most wonderful days of KEYEMSEE.

Clinical @ Mangalore

The hostel itself was a great place. Its food was known all over Mangalore for its high quality. Once a month, they had a special dinner and many students studying at the Regional Engineering College at Suratkal, close to Mangalore, would try to get invited to this dinner. In fact, another cousin of mine, who used to study there, would always make it a point to come to this dinner as my guest every month. Those were the days when we got 200 Rupees from home every month; we had to pay the mess bill and survive the rest of the month on whatever was left. Many of us were smokers at that time, and for a few days after the money came, we would smoke only Wills filter cigarettes, soon to shift to Charminar in the middle of the month, and then to half Charminar cigarettes. This would soon be replaced by the famous Mangalore Ganesh *beedies* till the next allowance came. The clinical section was very interesting compared to the preclinical boring routine. We walked from the hostel to the Wenlock Hospital nearly 2 km away every morning, from there back to the hostel for lunch, and then back again to the college and another 2 km for the theory classes and practical sessions. Many students had motorbikes and scooters, which lined the entire corridor of the ground floor. Occasionally, we would be lucky to get a lift from one of these people going to the hospital. We walked around Mangalore with great pride with the white coat, with the stethoscope casually dangling over one shoulder, and the knee hammer and a pen torch jutting out of our pockets. Standing around outside the hospital, we were the envy of the local arts college boys and girls.

We had many famous professors who taught us in those three years; some excellent teachers, and many outstanding clinicians. I'm reminded of two of my professors, specifically the Professor of Therapeutics KesavaPai, who was a MRCP and spoke often with a British accent. On my first day in the clinic in his ward, I was asked by him to examine a patient who had a bloated abdomen and he showed us how to place the fingers below the right rib and asked the patient to take a deep breath, and he said, see if you can feel anything. I did as I was told and felt something pushing past my finger as he took a deep breath. "Did you feel anything my boy?" he asked. "Yes," I said something pushed past my finger. "That, my boy is what we here in Mangalore call the liver. I don't know what you people in Manipal call it." That then was the first introduction to this great clinician. He would often wander into the ward early morning, stand at one end and say, "I can smell amoebiasis." Whether he could indeed, smell amoebiasis, which was so common in Mangalore, or whether it was a wild guess, I never knew, but we always found someone with amoebiasis in that ward. On one occasion, he asked a friend of mine some clinical question, which we did not answer correctly, and he asked him, "Did you know Robert Louis Stevenson, my boy," and when my friend said he did not, he said, "Thank God for that, because Stevenson wrote the article 'My travels with a donkey,' and I thought he was talking about you." He had this sarcastic sense of humor, which was unique to him, and I was to bump into this on more than one occasion.

Similarly, in surgery, we had an excellent surgeon and teacher called Prof Srinivasan. He too had his own way of making something understood and made surgery look simple and straightforward. Incidentally, during that time I myself had an attack of a cute appendicitis and was taken to this same Dr Srinivasan who did operate on me.

I was posted in Prof Srinivasan's unit and very quickly became a great fan.

We were a small group posted in his unit, and also a few other stragglers who walked in for Prof MS's ward classes. He picked out one from the crowd (now I haven't the faintest clue who it was) and asked him to examine the patient in the bed next to where we were all standing. He said, "Ten Minutes! Others come with me." He took the rest of us to another patient at the other end of the ward and took a discussion for exactly ten minutes. We all marched back to the first patient. The Professor put his arm around the person about to present that case and said, "Yes brother (he called every one brother), you have fifteen minutes to tell me everything about this case," emphasizing the word 'everything' while he had a sly grin on his face as he looked around at us. "The patient is a moderately built and nourished male, aged fifty-five years….," he started and went on to discuss the complaints, the various histories, etc. When he reached Differential Diagnosis, my Professor said, "Go On." Nobody else said anything. The boy went on with investigations, diagnosis, etc.. He looked expectantly at the Professor. "What?" he asked." "Peptic ulcer," the boy said. He continued on to treatment, prognosis, and stopped. "Describe the procedure," Prof. said with a straight face. Suddenly, he looked at his watch and said, "Stop! Your time is up. Do you have anything else to say?" The boy shook his head. We were all wondering why he was not interrupted nor was any discussion taking place during the presentation of the case.

The Professor went to the boy, put his arm on his shoulder and said, "Brother! You examined this patient for ten minutes and explained everything for fifteen minutes. In the last fifteen minutes, only the sex of the patient you said correctly! Everything else was humbug." Angrily, he turned to the rest of us and said, "I want each of you to examine this patient again for five minutes in the side room for five minutes, one at a time without talking to each other. I will be in the room watching you. I don't want history, etc. No talking to the patient."

When everyone had finished, he said we would discuss this case the next day. The next day he came into the ward in a bad mood (which was not very common) and said, "I am ashamed of this group." He looked at the patient and said, "*Lungi matha* underwear *thegiri*" (translation—remove your lungi and underwear), and there was this huge hernia, hydrocele, which none of us had seen.

We learned our lesson that day to examine the entire patient and not just what he complained about. Even today, it is ingrained into my head though as an ophthalmologist my patients may consider me a freak if I asked them to remove their clothes (that too in a dark room!).

Yet over these years, in at least a dozen difficult and complex cases, I have got a clue on examining the entire body, finding a swollen lymph node or a skin lesion, or an enlarged liver, which put me in the right direction to a diagnosis.

Clinical medicine was good fun followed by theory classes in these subjects; we also had to study nonclinical subjects like Pharmacology, Pathology, Forensic Medicine, Bacteriology, and Preventive Medicine.

We had an excellent Microbiology Professor called Dr Ananthakrishnan, and I think he went on to write a textbook also. He took special classes for our batch in small groups and made us make mug up Microbiology and made it seem to be such an easy subject so much so that by the time we went to the exam we had learned everything by heart, very much like my friends in Ernakulum who by hearted the

Louis Braille biography. The other subjects were tough and the problem was that many of them had to be written together so we had large portions to study for each of these exams. We didn't have so many medicines or drugs to study in Pharmacology those days. The practicals, however, were rather fascinating because we had to make solutions of different percentages, we had to learn how to pack powders in paper packets, and how to make the dosage markers, which were stuck to the clear glass bottles in which medicines were dispensed to patients (I'm sure most people today will not even know what I'm talking about). I liked forensic medicine; in fact, at one time, I almost thought of taking up the postgraduation in forensic medicine, had it not been my obsession for ophthalmology. I loved to by heart legal language and even today can recall without referring to anything the definition of rape that I read in the textbook of Forensic Medicine by Modi. "Rape in India is defined as the unlawful carnal knowledge by a man of a woman below the age of sixteen with or without her consent or above the age of sixteen when consent has been obtained by illegal means," so on and so forth (this of course has been totally changed now to a more explicit and detailed definition). I studied Modi's textbook of Forensic Medicine from cover to cover (or so I thought) while most of my friends or almost all my friends read forensic medicine from a red colored Guide to Forensic Medicine by Bhattacharya, which listed out everything in point form. When we went to the exam in Forensic Medicine, the first question said 'describe '*Defloration*' and the signs and symptoms.' I had absolutely no clue what this meant. In desperation, I made a sign language gesture to my friend sitting beside me in the examination hall; he understood what I was trying to say and signaled back a vulgar gesture, which I had no difficulty in deciphering. After the exam, when I went and checked I found that in the guide the relevant chapter started with the words, "Loss of virginity' (defloration) can happen because of...,' and so while in Modi after several pages of discussion on loss of virginity there were three words at the end of the chapter that said loss of virginity is also called defloration, and obviously the cover to cover reading had missed these words. My greatest thrill during this time was that I was getting to do ophthalmology for the first time and this is what I had joined medical college for. By coincidence the day I was posted with a few of my friends in the ophthalmology outpatient, we got a new and dynamic lecturer in ophthalmology. Dr C R Kamath had just returned from the UK having completed his diploma in London and joined the college as a lecturer in ophthalmology. He had a very charming personality always, immaculately dressed, spoke excellent English and many other languages, and could shift from one language to another without batting an eyelid. He had imported a brand new Fiat car, which he had brought back from the UK, which was the envy of all in the hospital parking lot. He carried this beautiful briefcase with foam cut outs for his ophthalmoscope, retinoscope, tonometer, eye drops, et cetera, and at that time, he seemed to be everything that an ophthalmologist should be. He was the first to teach me that the word ophthalmology had an H after the P. He was an excellent teacher making clinical ophthalmology simple and straightforward. We also had this is very senior doctor called Dr Narayanan Rao as a Professor in that subject. Between them, my interest in ophthalmology was strengthened. I took extra effort to study that subject, eventually landing me with the Narayana Rao Gold medal in the fourth MBBS year for being the highest scorer in ophthalmology (Incidentally, that was the first of forty-three other Gold medals I received in the course of my career in ophthalmology). This of course helped me get my postgraduate seat at a later date. I would go and attend every one of the ophthalmic theatres and was fascinated by the surgery and the results that it seemed to produce. We left pathology, pharmacology, ophthalmology, and forensic behind and moved on to the final year with Medicine Surgery, Obstetrics and Gynecology, and Preventive Medicine on the last lap of our journey into the MBBS. We worked very hard reading late into the night, often going out with my roommate Viji for a walk into town to drink a cup of tea at a shop near the bus stand in Mangalore and then walking back fully refreshed to continue reading for another couple of hours before we woke up and went about our daily routines. So, we wrote the theory papers, two for each subject, and then waited for practical exam dates to be announced. My problem with the kidney continued and very often while walking to the exam I would ask Viji or my other roommate Romani to discuss something about the kidney till we reached the exam hall. Finally, it became time for our practicals, and first I had my medicine practicals. There was a saying in the hostel that if you went to the medicine practical exam and found Professor Kesava Pai as the examiner and you got a kidney case, then you had already failed even before you started because he had his own classification of kidney disease and its management. As I went to my practicals, I realized that he was indeed the internal examiner with three other external examiners. I was given an emaciated looking man, which was allotted by the draw of lots. As was customary, I gave this man the two rupees that we gave all these patients before examining them so that they would cooperate (if not they would not even give you a proper history). I then began to talk to this guy in *Malayalam*, the native language of the neighboring state of Kerala from where he had come. At the end of taking down his history, I realized that I had no clue about what was wrong with him and my luck the patient volunteered saying "Doctor, I think there is something wrong with my urine because everybody has asked for it the previous two days of the exam. I have therefore kept some in the bottle below the bed." I knew then that I was in trouble here as it was a kidney case with Kesava Pai hovering around; what would I do not now? Since time was running out, I had to take the urine and examine it to do the various tests before my specified time of forty-five minutes was over. In the process of trying to reach this little bottle with urine under the bed, I knocked the bottle over and spilt most of the urine. I ran the end of the ward with what little I had and did test for albumin and did some microscopy and realized I did not have enough urine to do a test for sugar nor check the specific gravity. I had no alternative but to return to the bed and complete writing what I had done so far. From the other end of the ward, Dr K Kesava Pai shouted at the top of his voice to me "have you finished Rajendran?" he asked. When I nodded my head, he came to me with one of the external examiner and said, "I don't want all your stories, first give me your diagnosis, and in three minutes you prove it. If you do, you will pass, if not you will fail," and he said "Q E D" with a flourish, words that he used often and we knew it meant quite easily done. I don't remember exactly what the diagnosis was nor how I went about proving but I do know one of the things in the end was examination of the urine. And so I said albumin was present in microscopic findings and Kesava Pai said, "Stop, haven't you forgotten something?" I realized then that he meant the sugar because while talking about examining urine, it was customary to describe the color especially gravity the albumin sugar and microscopy in that order. "I did not have enough urine sample to check specific gravity or the sugar," I mumbled. Very politely, he asked me how I would test for urine sugar. And I said 5 ml of Benedict solution, add eight drops of urine, and heat and depending on the color change we could know if there was sugar or not. He asked if it was possible to do with 2.5 ml of Benedict solution and I said probably. He looked at me strangely and said in a voice that everybody in the hall could hear, "If you squeezed his penis you would have got four drops urine!" I was sure that I would have to see a repeat medical posting for another six months. Luckily for me, the afternoon session went off better than expected; the two short cases were very easy and I had done very well and in them as well. In fact, I was very surprised during the viva when Kesava Pai told the other external examiner with him "Babu is one of our bright students." This meant that I scraped through my medicine exam. The rest of the subjects I passed creditably and eventually I passed my MBBS with flying colors and missed the blue ribbon of the college (overall performance from the first year to the last) probably by a few marks. In any case, I was ready to go out into the real world of patients.

Internship/Senior House Surgeon

A Clinic and a Marriage, All within a year

Before I was let loose on the unsuspecting patients of the real world, it was required, as it is even today, that we do one year of internship or House surgery or hands-on-training before we got the license to practice. At that time, there was a rule that we could go and do the house surgery anywhere else as long as we did the three months of Community and Preventive Medicine in the state of Karnataka. A few of us then decided to come and try whether we could do our house urgency in Madras. Unfortunately, for us, the political situation here was undergoing a slight change and none of the decision-making ministers were available to confirm our place of work. After a few days in order not to waste more time, I decided to go back and finish my house urgency at Mangalore itself. However, returning to Mangalore through Bangalore, a friend of ours suggested that we try to do the house urgency in Bangalore instead because I could stay at home with my family. At that time my dad, my grandmother, and brother and sister were living in a house in Bangalore. So, I tried, and to my luck, and within two days I managed to get a posting at a government hospital in Bangalore. While the house urgency was a duration of twelve months with three months each of medicine, Surgery, and Obstetrics and Gynecology, the remaining three months were the Community and

Preventive Medicine. The government however said that the Community and Preventive Medicine could not be done in the government hospital, and so we went and got permission to do that at a private medical college. We chose to do that at the end of my internship. In two days, again I was asked to join duty starting with an afternoon shift in the casualty department. It was there that I met Dr Jagannath who was also joining the same day for his internship. Though I had not met him before, we hit it off very well from the very first day and today he continues to be one of my closest friends. We were posted under the supervision of a doctor, Kumar, who was an assistant surgeon grade in government service. Dr Kumar turned out to be an excellent guide for the two of us and became a very good friend as well. Casualty duty in the government hospital meant a couple of attempted suicides, usually consumption of some pesticide, and the whole lot of old asthma patients, some of them in rather severe conditions. There were of course the occasional cuts and bruises, patients with fever, and very rarely the occasional broken bone. In the beginning, I used to get worried saying these patients were being brought after consuming pesticide, but the casualty attenders and nurses did not seem to be bothered much about these cases. To the best of my knowledge, I don't think we lost a single patient in the three months that I was in the casualty. As soon as a poisoning case came, they were placed on a table that was placed next to the sink with the foot end up, a gastric tube was inserted and connected to the tap, and water was rushed into the abdomen. Within no time at all, the ingested material would come gushing out and would be replaced a little later by beaten egg albumin (which the patients' relatives had to supply). Of course, we had to take other symptomatic measures and treat them with a drip, and very often with Atropine injections. A few hours later, these people would be shifted to the ward where they probably were discharged in a day or two; however, these being medicolegal cases, the hold-up was that they had to be kept till the police investigated and gave clearance that they could be discharged. We had our own share of suturing and bandaging to do every day during our duties. But the worst situations were where the severe asthmatics who came by the hoards and lay in the corridor outside the casualty throughout the night and come back every couple of hours for repeated injections to control their wheezing. Most of these patients were new and so we had to decide what medicine worked best for them; and then, there were those who would walk into the casualty and say give me adrenaline or aminophylline or steroid, but more often than not the casualty ward boys and the nursing aide knew what exactly to give them because they were regulars. We were then shifted to do night duty in the casualty for another fifteen days before we were shifted out to regular duties. Unfortunately, my next duty was in what was called the injection rooms. This consisted of giving 200 to 300 injections to patients who stood outside the room and are sent by their physician or surgeon instructing which injection they were supposed to have. Most often, it used to be Penicillin or some form of it like long-acting Penicillin, Streptomycin, which was given for tuberculosis, and rarely antirabies injections and anti-tetanus toxoid (ATT). There were couple of saucepans in which the glass syringes and barrels were boiling continuously and a few in which the needles were continuously boiling; the nurses loaded these syringes and handed it to me and I just kept injecting these guys and women as they walked into the room with their arm ready for the injection. Another nurse or ward boy applied a dab of spirit over the site of injection. This was such a monotonous and often boring job, and usually by the end of the morning, we would all be smelling of Penicillin or some other medicine like the spirit from the swab.

Placement after that with a regular medical unit was much better, under an excellent cardiologist, in whose unit I was posted for medicine and was followed by a surgery posting that was also very interesting because of the dynamic head of surgery in whose unit I had the good fortune to work. By rotation, I was sent to the minor OT and got to do several circumcisions, hundreds of corn removals, ear lobe repairs, etc. In the septic OT, I must have done another hundred incisions and drainage of an abscess. Because of my interest in ophthalmology, by request, I got to do fifteen days of my surgical posting in the eye department. This unit was headed by Dr Like; my Prof Dr Kamath had also returned from the UK and was working in this hospital as one of the two consultant ophthalmologists. He was the most organized and systematic person I have ever seen. When he put on the white coat in the hospital to replace the jacket he was wearing, you could check your watch and it would be 8 am without fail. He was an excellent surgeon and it was a treat to sit in his outpatient and watch him at work. Over a hundred patients turned up every morning and patiently waited to be seen by him. He had this system of having two rows of benches, one on either wall in his OPD, and the men sat on one of these benches and the women on the opposite bench. Without breaking the order, he would see one male patient followed by one female patient, and irrespective of who you are, if you wanted to see him in this government hospital, you had to come in this line and take your turn. In between his patients, probably every twenty or twenty-five patients, he would go into the side room where they would have kept patients for checking the intraocular pressure using the Shiotz tonometer, seeing the fundus of dilated patients, and about ten or fifteen patients for lacrimal probing including young children. It was fascinating to watch him do this probing because never have I seen him withdraw the probe (except to remove it) even once and we just watched the probe going straight down the nasolacrimal duct and come out through the nose. He was a great surgeon and did very clean and quick surgeries. I had to leave the eye department when I had to complete the remaining postings. The remaining week of my surgical posting, I had to do anesthesia where a very jolly and very efficient anesthetist would allow me to hold the mask and press the bag once the patient was settled down. Most of the cases were done under open ether. The last and final clinical posting was in Obstetrics and Gynecology, and to my bad luck, I was posted in the unit of the most ferocious woman in the hospital. I noticed that the entire staff including those doctors doing senior house surgeons and even the government assistant surgeons were mortally afraid of her because she would shout and scream at everybody. She was a great surgeon and the word was that she was very gifted and could deliver babies normally even in the most complex situations. She was also extremely kind to her patients, often giving them money to buy medicines. On the very first day with her, within half an hour of my joining her unit, she charged into the ward and seeing me standing with nothing to do asked if I was the new intern. When I just nodded, she said, "Oh are you dumb also or just pretending?" Then she said go and get the D&C patient ready in the minor OT (Minor Operation Theatre) and off she went on her rounds. I asked the only nurse left in the ward where her minor OT and who the D&C patient was. Luckily, she sent a ward boy with me and by the time she reached the OT, the patient was on the table. She looked at her watch and asked if the anesthetist had come and I said I hadn't seen him. By now, she was livid, and just to keep her mind off the situation, I asked her if I could position the patient with the legs in the stirrup, and she glared at me and said, "Shut up! Go find the anesthetist." I did that and found he was busy since the case he was doing hadn't finished. By now, I was mortally afraid to give her this news. From a phone outside the OT, I rang the minor OT and told the nurse who answered about the delay. I gave her a few minutes to calm down and then went back into the OT. She asked me what posting I had done before coming here and I said "anesthesia." She said, "Then you give the general anesthesia, let's see what you have learned." I was petrified. She glared at me and said, "I want her under in five minutes." I quickly recalled the ethyl chloride and then the ether being poured over a mask held over the nose and mouth, and while the nurse and theatre boy held the patient's legs and arms, I kept pouring the ether. Soon, she became quiet, and even before I said anything, the doctor was cleaning and draping her. She did not use the stirrups at all. The nurse just folded the legs and placed the feet apart on the OT table itself. The doctor sat at the foot end of the table on a low stool. As the doctor started her D&C, the patient made a few groaning sounds. From down the other end of the table, I heard the doctor say, "Make her deeper." More ether on the mask, and the patient settled down. A few minutes later, from the head end I was not sure if the patient was breathing. I tried to feel the pulse and did not find any either. In total panic, I left the mask and moved to the side to check her pulse properly; suddenly the patient took a deep breath just as the doctor was beginning the curettage. Before I knew what happened, the patient gave a mighty scream and pushed out her legs in the process knocking this famous big time gynecologist right off the stool and onto the floor in the corner of the Operation Theatre. Luckily, for me, the scheduled anesthetist walked into the theatre, saw the confusion, and told me to leave. The gynecologist wanted to suspend me for a week or shift me out of the unit, but the anesthetist pacified her and asked me to go and apologize to her in her clinic, and so was avoided a major disaster. A few days later, she surprisingly said she should never have asked me to start the case, and thankfully, the matter ended there. The remaining portion of the three months was a nightmare but I survived and got out alive and in one piece, I must say. Jaggu and I then rushed off to our Community Medicine posting. That was really a big letdown after all the hectic workload in the previous three months. But it did give Jaggu and me a lot of free time to hatch a plan to start a small clinic near the house where we stayed in the eastern part of Bangalore. We rented a room adjoining a small grocery shop. The room probably measured about ten feet by eight feet and protruding from this was a smaller extension measuring about four feet by six feet. We spent all of four hundred rupees, that is two hundred each, investing in this clinic. One day, we both went to Spencers on M G Road and bought large bottles containing concentrates of the commonly used mixtures of that time, Mixtura Alba, Carminative Mixture, and Soda Sal Mixture (this was a salicylate like Aspirin today I think) (I am sure few people will remember these. I myself am surprised that I remember). We had with time collected a large amount of physician's sample bottles of medicines and all these were tightly stored on a shelf in the extension. The extension itself was separated by a curtain from the other room, which was the consultation room, which had two tables and chairs plus an examination bed, all taken on hire.

The clinic was named after our mothers, and was hence called Devi Rajam Clinic, and we had a large board outside displaying this. Incidentally, the board was the costliest thing in that clinic. Like the government hospital injection room, we too had a saucepan with boiling syringes, needles, and barrels. By consensus, we agreed that the only injection we would give was Terramycin, which we knew was very safe. We never even kept Penicillin in the clinic. Of course, asthma medicines and the occasional ATT, which we stored in the shop fridge next door. We had a small boy who worked for the shop to clean and open this clinic every evening. The boy made sure that only one attendant came with the patient for want of space inside. Very optimistically, we even made some serially numbered tokens, which the boy was to distribute to the patients as they arrived so that they were seen in that order except for emergencies. I do not think we had to use those tokens except on a very few days. When a patient did come, we took turns to examine them alternatively and then had a joint consultation in the side room deciding which of the three mixtures we had to give. Portions of these mixtures were mixed with tap water and dispensed in bottles the patient bought. Occasionally, if the patient looked very sick, we would add a lavish portion of the physician sample, like Crocin, into the mixture when we dispensed it. We were good at cutting the dosage markers and proudly stuck them on these bottles, and I think many patients from nearby slums were sent to us because of that, since other doctors told them to take one teaspoon or something!! We would stay in the clinic till about 9 pm even if there were no patients. We charged two rupees for a consultation and three if we dispensed medicine (provided they bought the bottle, if not, that was fifty paisa extra). If we gave an injection that was three rupees extra.

One day, we got a stunning looking young woman, who walked into the clinic and wanted to know if we would give her Streptomycin injections for a month since she was here on a holiday and had to take this without fail. Of course, we said yes. But, we had two issues, one how much to charge for the injection alone since there was no consultation and she brought the medicine. We decided three rupees would be okay per injection. My goodness, how many movies we could see we thought. But we went out and said four rupees, but since you will come for a month, we will give you a discount so give us hundred rupees in advance instead of hundred and twenty (we wanted to get the money in advance in case she decided to go elsewhere in between the treatment); she pulled out a thick wad of notes and Jaggu and I glared at each other because we could have said ten rupees each and she would have paid. We told her that she needed to take the injection on her hips and she said she already knew that and that she would come from the next evening in a more comfortable dress to start the course. We now had the second issue to resolve between the two of us. Who would give the injection? Finally, we reached a compromise. One day, one person would give the injection, while the other rubbed the spirit, and the next day the roles would be reversed. After a few days, she said she would like Jaggu to give the injection; so I ended up rubbing spirit and rubbing the injection site after it was done. I was not going to grumble or object to this arrangement.

On the few days that we did make some money, we went to my house and had dinner and were off to the movies on Jaggu's Jawa motorcycle. Rarely, we made enough money to take even my brother and sister to the movies.

When both us eventually got PG seats and left Bangalore, we sold the clinic to a friend for 800 rupees making a hundred percent profit on our investment in just a few months, a great deal even by any standard!

It was fun while it lasted.

The Community Medicine postings got over; we had to go back to the college to get our completion certificates. We now had some time before applying for postgraduation. Jaggu wanted to do anesthesia and I of course did not waver from ophthalmology. In the meantime, both of us applied for and got positions as Senior House surgeons. Jaggu, I think in anesthesia and me in ophthalmology. This was again a fun period of my life. I was doing exactly what I wanted in ophthalmology, and running the clinic with Jaggu in the evenings. It was a totally stress-free period. I had to go to the Mysore University convocation to pick up my degree and then ran around to register in The Karnataka Medical Council while waiting for the PG admissions to be called.

On 6 September 1971, in the ancestral home of my future in-laws, I got engaged to Giri.

On 7 January 1972, I lost my bachelor status in return for which, I got this incredible girl called Giri, as my wife, the daughter of a very senior technocrat, Mr Nayar, in the rubber industry in Madras and his wife Rajam. In fact, it was he who started manufacturing the famous MM FOAM brand of foam rubber mattresses and pillows in India. Their family and my family were very close friends in Colombo, and Giri was just a year older to and a good friend of my sister. It was a very grand wedding in a hall called the Abbotsbury, where the present Hyatt hotel in Chennai stands. Anyone who was anybody in Madras was there for the morning wedding and or the evening reception the same evening. The next day, my wife and I left on a short honeymoon to a place called Coonoor on the Ghats. We returned to Bangalore and Chennai where Giri continued with her final year of her BA degree course at Stella Maris College. I returned to the routine of Senior House Surgency. Giri has been beside me for better or for worse; for richer, for poorer; in sickness and in health; to love and to cherish from that day onward for the next forty-four years. She has borne our two fantastic children, Priya, a British citizen now, living in London, and Sushil, an Australian citizen (since he was born in Melbourne while I trained there), now living with his beautiful and caring wife Serena and their most wonderful two young girls, Maya and Amita.

Neither of my children opted to follow me in the medical profession. The first few months of married life were taken away by the thought of getting or not getting the postgraduation seat that I wanted. I had applied to the Minto Hospital in Bangalore and waited for the application to be called at other places. My father-in-law had a backup plan for me to go work at a very famous Eye Institute in Kerala close to a town where his brother worked and therefore knew the chief there. He was told I was welcome, but to first try and finish my PG, and then go there to gain experience. This sounded more logical and I was planning towards that goal. Suddenly one day, my friend called and said the call had been made for the PG seats and that it would be better if I went personally in the next few days and completed the formalities of submission of my application.

Postgraduation

OEU Institute, Manipal

I applied for PG in ophthalmology. At that time, the PG application at the Kasturba Medical College was only two rupees each and it was customary for everyone to apply for five to ten courses. I paid my two rupees and applied for only DOMS (**D**iploma in **O**phthalmic **M**edicine and **S**urgery). I later found out that the college had applied for Master of Surgery (MS) recognition and were awaiting permission. I was asked to make an application for that but they could not accept the two rupees since the course had not yet been advertised nor recognized. In fact, I applied for my dream qualification without charge. I got selected for the diploma course and joined it at KMC Mangalore back with Prof Narayana Rao and Dr C.R.Kamath.

Within a few days, the MS got sanctioned and I was reregistered as the first MS postgraduate in Manipal in ophthalmology under Dr P.N. Srinivasa Rao. The very first day that I went to meet him and joined as a student, he had just left the OPD and was walking towards his house for lunch. I ran behind him and asked to speak to him for a few minutes. He turned around quite irritated that somebody had probably dared to stop him and asked me rather angrily, "Who are you?" I introduced myself and told him that I was the new MS postgraduate student and had been asked to join his department in Manipal. He seemed quite angry and said that he knew nothing about it and therefore I was to go back and join Mangalore till somebody told him what was happening. I had no option but to do as he said, but since I had left Bangalore, gone to Mangalore, and now to Manipal carting my luggage with me, and now I did not want to go back to Mangalore the same afternoon. So, I went to the room of a friend of mine and stayed in with him for the day. Early next morning, I went to Mangalore and met Prof Narayanan Rao and explained what had gone on and told him to please ring up the Dean at Manipal, Dr Srinivasan Rao, so that I would be allowed to join there. By noon that day, I was back at Manipal and decided that I would go and see the Dean first, which on looking back I should have probably done in the first place, to get a letter from him before seeing Dr Srinivasan Rao. So, I got a letter from the Dean and waited till the next morning because I did not want to confront Dr Srinivasan Rao in the corridor or on the road again. The next morning, when I knew that he was in the outpatient department, I met him in his cabin and gave him the letter given from the Dean. He was a totally different person that morning and welcomed me into his department. At that time, I did not realize that I was his first postgraduate because I thought he already had diploma students training with him. It was indeed a learning experience for both of us. For Professor as a postgraduate teacher and for me as a postgraduate student.

He was an extremely tough task master and expected you to be thorough in what you dealt with and told me on the very first day that this was a postgraduate course and that nobody would spoon-feed me and that I had to learn on my own, by my own hard work, and that if I had any doubt or any difficulty at any time, I was free to approach him. He was relieved to know that I was a student of Manipal, and so did not have to take me around the library and other facilities. He introduced me to the rest of the staff consisting of a few optometrists and two nursing aides. While Dr Srinivasan Rao saw patients in his cabin, I sat at a table placed outside his room. Patients who came with their records were seen by the optometrists and then the files were placed on my table. Having worked as a senior house surgeon for nearly six months in Bangalore, I was quite aware of how to work up a case in the OPD. So, I sort of slipped into the groove quite easily and saw these cases, which were then sent to the Professor. Very often, he would find something wrong with what I had written and he would call me in and explain what was wrong and what to do about it. I do not ever recall him calling me and congratulating me about something good that I had done. The department also had many inpatients admitted in different wards of the hospital. We had a theatre, which we shared with the general surgeons on specific days. Next to the theatre was the postoperative ward, where patients remained for a few hours before being sent to their regular ward. Every morning, exactly at 8 am, we began rounds. Just Professor and me from the postoperative ward. We probably had, at that time, about twenty patients admitted for different reasons when we started our rounds; from the first week onwards, he expected me to have at my fingertips all the details about all the patients admitted under his care. These rounds took about an hour or a little more and after the first month the walk in between the wards were usually a dressing down that I got for any acts of omission or commission. After three months, I got some help in the form of doctor Shoba, who was already a diploma holder in ophthalmology from Mangalore being, posted to Manipal as the second MS candidate. She being a diploma holder and sitting at the same table as me, in the outpatient, I could ask and clarify my doubts with her rather than having to go in to the Professor's cabin very often. Even then, when we sent a file, on rare the occasions, with a wrong entry or a wrong diagnosis for the Professor's opinion and final disposal, some of these case sheets were thrown over the divider of his cabin and would land on the table where we sat much to the shock of the patients sitting beside us. On such occasions, we knew that either one or both of us were going to get a piece of his mind. In those days, indirect ophthalmoscopy and minor procedures like begonioscopy were significant major events in the department and it was only after a few months that we were allowed to handle these instruments and equipment. We also had to assist him in the theatre cases. Being a very short-tempered person, he could flare-up at the smallest misdeed, especially in the theatre. And therefore, those of us in the nursing staff and we the doctors, were doubly careful while assisting him in his cases. He was an extremely talented and gifted surgeon and had outstandingly good surgical results. There was no surgery that he would not undertake as far as ophthalmology was concerned. What he didn't know, he learned from the library and from his colleagues and ventured into the various subspecialties of today. He was doing ab interno sections using the Graefe knife and switched to ab externo technique using the Keratome and Bard Parker blade so that it was easier to teach this students the surgical skills of doing cataract surgery, starting with me. At that time, we also had started to do eye camps in and around Manipal. These camps were held in conjunction with various Rotary and Lions Clubs and varied in distance from 50 km to over several hundred kilometers away from Manipal. If the camps were further away, then we stayed there for a few days, and after the surgeries, the main team returned, leaving behind a senior and junior postgraduate to look after the postop patients. It was in these camps that both Shoba and I were given increasingly different tasks to perform first by giving the blocks (giving the local anesthetic injections) and later to make the conjunctival flap, then the corneal section, removal of the lens, and suturing, in that order. I'm sure many surgeons may not remember the very first solo surgery they did. But, I do not only remember the first, but the second as well, and this is because of a strange coincidence. We had in our unit a senior nurse called Meenakshi. In one of the camps where I was asked or rather allowed to do my first solo cataract, the patient who I was operating was called Meenakshi, and it so happened that this nurse was assisting me. To add to the coincidence, the second case that I did once again the same day assisted by Meenakshi was called Babu. And therefore, I can't forget these two names. The cases went off very well, adding to my confidence to do more and more surgeries over time. We had camps where we operated from fifty cases at one camp to three hundred cases in a different camp. Dr Srinivasan Rao never took lecture classes for us, but we learned by his discussions and his intensive questioning each and everything that we did. He had this very peculiar habit of being in the library till eight o'clock in the evening and watched us also in the library. And just as he was leaving, he would go to the librarian and check what books Shoba and I had taken to read. The next day, sure enough he would quiz us on the topics that appeared in those books, whether it is a squint book, retina book, a surgery book, et cetera. In those days of course, other than the several volumes of Duke Elder, the next big ophthalmic book was Sorsby in four volumes. I still recall, once he gave me an assignment to discuss retinal detachment and its management. He gave me three days; these were long before the days of "*googling*" so I referred to Stalard's textbook of Ophthalmic Surgery or some other book that covered retinal surgery. I wrote what I thought were the basic requirements in retinal surgery, identify the hole, do diathermy, or cryo to seal the hole, drain the fluid, and apply a buckle to release the traction. This much I had elaborated and presented it him during the discussion.

Dr Srinivasa Rao had done a Commonwealth Fellowship in retinal surgery with the famous Dr Fison in the UK and so was quite strong in surgery of the retinal as it existed at that time. But, when I gave him this presentation, even to this day I have no idea why he tore up the piece of paper and said "Rubbish" and walked out. Looking back, even today the principal of retinal surgery other than vitrectomy covers only the features that I have already mentioned. He had an uncanny knack for diagnosis and therapy, his clinical acumen was *par excellence,* and of his ophthalmology colleagues from around the state referred cases to him for his final opinion. In that way, we learned a great deal by seeing a large variety of cases and how to handle complex and difficult cases, both the disease and the patient.

While it is impossible to discuss individual patients in this book, I still recall a particular young boy whom I will refer to as Prabhu. This eleven-year-old boy was brought to the OPD by his father complaining that the boy was not able to see properly. He had been brought by bus from a neighboring village. When I asked the father how long he had this problem for, he said from the previous night; when we checked his vision though, he seemed to have about 50% of vision both for distance and near. The boy as such had no other complaint when I examined him; we could find absolutely nothing wrong with the sight nor the retina and optic nerve even after we examined him after dilating the pupil. I took the father aside and tried to get a little more history about the complaint. I asked him how the boy was in his studies, what class he was studying, et cetera. The father said that the boy was a very good student and scored high marks in all subjects except in Hindi. He said the boy found Hindi very difficult and did not like the subject at all; in fact, the father said that on that particular day when the boy was in eye OPD, he was supposed to be in the Hindi exam. Later, I took the boy aside and asked him some of the same questions, including whether he was missing the Hindi exam; he said he was, but if we gave a medical certificate, he would be exempt.

This got me thinking, and I thought to myself that I had made the brilliant diagnosis. I took the file to the Professor and explained the case in detail and showed him what I had written on the file with a diagnosis? Malingering. The Professor called the boy in and had another look at him in detail and told them to wait outside and gave me a big lecture. He said, "You have no business to diagnose malingering; if there is nothing in the eye, say so, and refer the patient to somebody else, like the neurologist or psychiatrist; we are not supposed to make diagnosis out of our area of specialization." He said to admit the boy and observe him for some time. So, I admitted him in the wards and got all the investigations and X-rays done; he was referred to the Neurologist and Psychiatrist, who found nothing wrong with him. At that time, there were also several Tamil-speaking laborers admitted in the ward who had eye injuries following some explosion in their factory. So, after admitting the young fellow, I told these Tamil workers, in their language, which the boy never understood, to keep an eye over this young chap and watch his movements whether he really couldn't see or whether he was pretending. The next morning, we came back and asked these people what they noticed; they said that he was walking around the ward for a few hours then had come and lay down and that he was still in bed. But, these people did not think that he could not see because he seemed to be walking in the ward quite comfortably. When I went to the boy and checked him again, I found no difference in his general condition. I then told him that he needed a few injections, which would make him better. I had prescribed some vitamin injection thinking that the pain of the many injections would force him come out of the malingering. The next day and the day after the situation continued exactly the same way, the boy saying he could not see but he would go and fetch his meals and eat it by himself, and a further recording of his vision showed it was still about 50% of normal. The injections obviously seemed to have no effect, so that was stopped. One evening, when I had gone for my rounds, the boy said he had a headache. I have him some Analgin tablet and went off duty. Little later in the night, the duty nurse called me and said that Prabhu was having severe headache with severe vomiting. I contacted the neurosurgeon who said to immediately repeat his skull X-ray. I went with Prabhu to Radiology; then we were shocked to find that he had a bled into a Cranioharyngioma, which had burst out of the pituitary's fossa causing his headache and vomiting. It appears, the neurosurgeon told me later, that probably the tumor fell back when he lay down and so got a little vision, but when he was upright it probably pressed on his optic nerve portion, the chiasma, in front of the tumor. Prabhu eventually underwent emergency craniotomy that night and had an eventful recovery. It was heartening to see him about three decades later on a visit to Manipal. The same Prabhu, now working in a local bank, had come to the eye department to get a pair of reading glasses. The paramedical in the department introduced him to me and explained to me who he was. Prabhu asked me how long I would be in Manipal, and when I said two days, he came back that evening to the hotel that I was staying with his father, wife, and two children, and explained to the children in front of me that it was I who saved his life (though I had nothing to do with that).

We traveled far and wide to do our camps, till subsequently the government changed the rule and said patients could be examined at camps but had to be brought to a base hospital for surgery. When he went out to those camps where we did surgery, it was a big event for two days before we left because of the amount of things that we had to pack and carry with us. I remember on one particular trip to a town faraway; about one hour in the bus dedicated for carrying us to camps, I casually asked the nurse whether she had Xylocaine injections with adrenaline as well as the plain Xylocaine; the nurse banged her head and suddenly remembered that they had left the Xylocaine back in the hospital. We suddenly made an excuse to stop the vehicle at a hotel on the pretext of wanting to have tea and some to use the toilet, because if the Professor had found out about the Xylocaine, all hell would have broken loose. From a phone in the hotel, we rang the department and asked them to send somebody with the Xylocaine by overnight bus, so as to reach the camp venue early morning. In these situations, we learned crisis management, and have found out that in later life we were able to handle a crisis with a calm mind. Two years into my course, I asked Professor whether I could write the diploma in ophthalmology exam so that I would have some exposure to an exam situation writing the MS later. But he insisted that I must go ahead and finish my MS in the three-year allotted to me. My thesis for my MS was "*Fascia Lata as a buckling material in retinal detachment Surgery.*" When a retinal detachment was posted for surgery at 9 am, I would enter the theatre at 8 am and help the plastic surgeon remove the fascia lata (this is a tough fascia covering the muscles of the thigh). Over a period of time, I was doing this on my own. Patients always complained more about the pain in the leg than in the operated eye. I soon realized that I could get fascia lata for three or four cases from each leg, and so we stopped removing it from every patient and stored the extra in vacuum bottles (prepared for us by the college of Pharmacy), with a few antibiotic drops under refrigeration. This was part of my thesis.

At that time, we had a state conference held in Manipal and Professor wanted me to read my thesis as a paper at that conference. I was not sure nor was he whether this was permitted, since the thesis had not yet been submitted and accepted. So, he asked me to go and find out from the head of the Urology Department, as he had people working under him who had submitted many theses. He asked me to go ahead and present it but not to use the same title as my thesis. The reason my Professor wanted me to present that paper was because he said people in the audience could ask questions and that it would give me an idea on what corrections had to be done before submission of my thesis. He then realized that there were a couple of very senior ophthalmologists attending the conference who were likely to sit in the audience and ask embarrassing questions of me while presenting the paper. Two days later, my Professor suggested that we make these difficult people as chairman and cochairman and make them sit on the stage so they may not continue to ask questions and may end with one or two. And that is what we did, which paid dividends because no one in the audience asked any questions neither the chairman nor the cochair, except one person in the audience asking what it looked like; luckily I had put a bottle of it in my pocket, which I proudly flashed before them. That was my very first experience at presenting the scientific paper. The thesis itself had to be typed and this was done regularly for all postgraduate students by the librarian of our college, who was aware of how these were supposed to be formatted. The problem was that if you made any significant change, the whole thing probably had to be typed all over again because the page formatting would change. Every time I showed my thesis in progress to my Professor, he refused to have a look at it and he said to get it corrected by the Head of the Urology department. I did this with great care and finally the Head of Urology said to go ahead and type it, as I didn't have much time left. I made one final attempt to show it to Professor, but he said, "If that fellow I said it is okay then it must be okay; you don't waste time; go ahead and type and bind it." I asked the librarian and since this was the first thesis being typed for the eye department, he said he would ask my Professor when he came to the library that evening; the next day the librarian told me that the Professor had said that he checked with the Head of Urology and he had said it was fine so to go ahead and complete. We had to make four copies of the thesis, which he had bound and delivered to me, and now I had to get the signature of the Professor on the thesis. I left all copies of the theses on his table as he had gone for lunch and I myself went out for lunch. When I came back, the optometrist told me that the Professor wanted to see me. It was a great trepidation that I entered to see him, because, in case he made some major changes, I did not have time to make four new copies in time for the submission, which meant that I would have lost six months. However, when I went in, all he asked was whether I was allowed to have one page, which was titled acknowledgments, and I had acknowledged his guidance and help and that of the Head of Urology. I said that I had checked some other theses in the library from the Urology department and they always had an acknowledgment page. That was the only comment he made about my thesis and immediately signed it, shook my hand, and said, "All the best."

Retinal surgery seemed to be an outstandingly difficult procedure to comprehend and to do in those days as Professor was trying to do retinal surgery using a direct ophthalmoscope in the theatre while he would have made a retinal using the indirect ophthalmoscope in the outpatient and in the ward. To keep the direct ophthalmoscope sterile, it was kept in a glass chamber containing formalin tablets and by the time we took the ophthalmoscope out and tried to keep it next to our eye to see the fundus, it caused a tremendous amount of eye irritation. The entire surgical procedure with a single and simple horseshoe tear would take anywhere from three to four hours. I was sure that there was an easier way to do this, and at the back of my mind, I decided that after my postgraduation I would try and do a Fellowship in retinal surgery somewhere preferably outside the country. While the exams were nearing, we heard that a classmate of my wife had gone with her husband to do some training in Melbourne, Australia. So, I told my wife one day to send a letter to her friend and ask her to find out the address of an eye hospital in Melbourne and send it to us. In those days, an aerogram would take anything from five days to three weeks to reach an overseas destination. After about two months, we got a reply from this girl with the address of the Royal Victorian Eye and Ear Hospital in East Melbourne. It appears, she herself had forgotten about this request, but one day their car broke down on the road and while waiting for it to be fixed she found that she was standing next to the Royal Victorian Eye and Ear Hospital and so copied down the address and sent it to us. I kept this address away because there was nothing I could do until I passed my MS. Finally, the theory exams commenced where we had four papers and the last paper for three hours had only one question, no choice just one question, which had to be answered in three hours. In my case, I got a brilliant question, because I had read up about it during my work on the thesis and the question was to discuss the use of human biological tissues in ophthalmology. I had finished writing this answer within ninety minutes, but the Dean who was supervising the postgraduate exam refused to let me go out of the hall. A few weeks after the theory exam, we had our practical exam. This was the first time that the practical exam was being held in Ophthalmology in Manipal. The Professor did not want to seem to have not prepared for this exam and therefore he called eighty-seven patients to come as patients to be examined by three candidates. Throughout the three years, I had noticed him writing file numbers in a small diary that he carried with him in his pocket not realizing that these were the interesting cases that he obviously wanted to call for the exam. We of course had no idea who these cases were because though we had seen them we had not kept a record about them. In addition to Shoba and myself, there was a third candidate appearing for the MS exam. He was already a diploma holder in Mangalore, and was a lecturer in the eye department in Mangalore. I was at a great disadvantage because I was not a diploma holder; Shoba was not only a diploma holder but pregnant and nearly full-term, while the third candidate had already appeared previously for the MS exam in Mangalore and failed. Statistically, I had therefore the least chance of passing because this was my first attempt and nor was I a diploma holder. We had three external examiners and Professor as the internal. Because it was the first exam, we also had an inspector and a very senior ophthalmologist from Bombay (Mumbai now), who I was not sure whether he was sent by the Medical Council of India (MCI) or the Mysore University.

Anyway, the inspector was not supposed to ask the candidates any question but he made a note of how the exam was being conducted in general, specifically the question asked by the examiners and answers given by the candidates and eventually carried the pass results with what he thought should have been the results. We had our practical long and short cases in the morning, apart from cases of refraction, which is a standard practice in all ophthalmic PG exams. In the afternoon, we had Microbiology, Pathology, Instruments, and viva. I had done fairly well in the morning and was quite confident about the afternoon session even before I went in to meet the examiners. After I finished the Microbiology, Pathology, and the Instruments, as I started my viva, we got word that Sheik Mujibur Rahman of Bangladesh had been assassinated (this was on August 15, 1975). The examiners then kept discussing within themselves about the troubles in Bangladesh and India's involvement in the creation of Bangladesh, et cetera; after about half an hour of the discussions, they suddenly realized that I was still in the hall and there were two more candidates to examine. They said, "Okay, you go and send the lady in." And that was how I passed my MS exam. One of the biggest obsessions of Professor was of people taking leave. He hated when people asked for leave and even more when they went on leave. I had a peculiar problem on that particular day. My brother who was working in Singapore was on his way to the US to do his masters had come to my house in Bangalore and wanted very much to see me and my young daughter. So, it was imperative that I leave Manipal to Bangalore that night after the exam. As the senior PG in the department, I was probably expected to organize these patients admitted for the exam to be discharged with proper instructions and probably to set right things in the OP, which had been rearranged for the exam. But, I was in no mood to go and ask the leave, as I was more tense to know how I had done in the exam. However, a friend of mine volunteered to go and find out about my leave as well as the result, as my wife and I were busy packing to go to Bangalore. Later that evening, he went to the Professor and got permission, who with great reluctance gave me permission to go and return in two days' time. When my friend asked him the results of the exam, he said sarcastically, "Those who have done well have passed." I was sure that those meant Shoba and the third candidate. But I had no option but to leave; but just as we were boarding the bus in Udipi to go to Bangalore, my friend came running and said that I had indeed passed. After my break in Bangalore, we came back to Manipal and I continued to do what I was doing till the official results came and then I was appointed as an Assistant Professor in the department.

Fellowship at Melbourne

While working as an Assistant Professor in Manipal, I remembered the address of the eye hospital in Melbourne and sent the application saying I would like to undergo a training in retinal surgery (vitreous surgery hadn't started then; hence, Vitreo retinal surgery, as it is called today, did not exist). I sent them all my relevant documents plus photographs of the cover, conclusion, and bibliography of my thesis (the portion that mentioned Crock et al.). As I had mentioned earlier, in those days, letters took three to four weeks to reach an overseas destination. About two months later, I received a letter from the Administrative Officer of the Eye and Ear Hospital saying they had received my letter but did not know what post I had applied for. He did mention that looking at my biodata it looked as if I wanted to apply for the post of Fellowship in retinal surgery. He said they had available a vacancy for an year-long International Fellowship in retinal surgery and that it would be advertised in the British Journal of Ophthalmology and to reapply at that time. I wrote back immediately to them that the Fellowship in fact was what I had in mind but did not know what it was called at their hospital. However, I said the British Journal of Ophthalmology came to our library by sea and took about six to eight months to reach us. Therefore, I requested that my previous letter itself be treated as an application for the International Fellowship. And then, I forgot about it. About three months later, I got a telegram from Melbourne saying I had been selected for the International Fellowship in that I had to join by the first week of April. I sent a telegram back saying I've accepted the offer but needed documentation of my selection with the terms and conditions so as to enable me to apply for my Australian Visa. Soon the formalities were all completed and I was ready to travel to Melbourne with my family (Priya my daughter had been born by then and was just three years old, my wife was expecting our second child.)

At the end of March, we decided to try and contact somebody in Melbourne who could meet and guide us on our arrival. My wife whose friend was in Melbourne and had sent us the address was back in Madras, so we asked, and she said she could call a doctor friend of theirs in Melbourne to help us. This was in March 1976, and we were in the period of urgency that was declared by the Prime Minister Mrs Indira Gandhi; this meant that making a foreign call was a very tedious process. We had to book the call two days in advance specifically giving the name of the person we were going to stick to and the duration of the call. We also specially had to specify in what language the conversation would take place and the operator mentions that the call would be terminated at the end of three minutes and also if at any time we chose to speak in some other language. My wife's friend came over to our house at the appointed time and did make a call to her doctor friend in Melbourne. Unfortunately, that doctor was traveling out of the state for a medical conference, but he assured us that somebody would meet us on arrival.

We left for Melbourne via Singapore and reached Melbourne on 3 April 1976 in a flight that had been delayed seven hours; in fact, the halt was in Sydney. I was sure that nobody was supposed to meet us as they would not have the patience to stay around for seven hours, and that we would not be received by anybody; surprisingly, when we came out of the airport, we found an Indian couple walking towards us, who later became our good friends. The woman seemed to be as pregnant or maybe a little more than my wife at that time. Due to the severe Reserve Bank of India restrictions current at that time, we were allowed only seven US dollars in foreign currency per head, which meant that when we went and landed in Melbourne we had US$ 21 between us; Mani and his lovely wife took us to a travel lodge in Carlton in Melbourne, which was close to the Eye and Ear hospital in East Melbourne. Knowing India's RBI restrictions, he enquired about the money I had; I told him about the twenty-one dollars I had. He explained that the travelers lodge did not require an advance, and that we had to pay only when we vacated the place. Mani showed me the way from the travelers lodge to the Eye hospital, which I had to join the next morning. With a little money that we had, we managed to buy milk and biscuits for our daughter.

The next morning, I went and reported for work at the eye and ear hospital. I went straight to the office looking for the Administrative Officer who I had been corresponding with. It turned out his name was Mr Landerman and he was an Anglo-Indian, originally from Madras and had migrated to Australia; he was very kind and understood my financial situation, and at our very first meeting, he said that I could speak to my Professor, and then having joined, could ask for an advance of my salary after a few days. He then took me around and showed me around the hospital and introduced me to Prof Gerard Crock. The first day that I met him, he said something and I said "Yes, sir," which was rather a surprise to him, and he said, "I haven't been knighted by her Majesty yet. So you please call me Gerard and I will call you Raj." We Indians are not used to calling our teachers by their first name and it seemed a rather difficult thing to do. Over the course of that day, we came to a compromise and I decided to call him as Professor. Prof Crock was a tall as me, an incredibly compassionate and kind human being.

He was internationally famous not only for his skill in ophthalmology but also for being the inventor of the Shultz Crock indirect ophthalmoscope. He was forever fiddling around innovating something or the other, and in fact, next to his room was a fully equipped workshop, in which a very able man called Jlubo who used to make things according to the Professor's direction. While I was there, I have seen the development of the COMMIDO indirect ophthalmoscope (**C**ombine **O**perating **M**agnifier and **M**iniature **I**ndirect **O**phthalmoscope), a unique contact lens corneal cuter, and the original set of Sutherland fVitreous Instruments. In fact, they did a great deal of basic research having their own research laboratory and even an electron microscope on that floor. I was introduced to the other people in the Department of Ophthalmology of the University of Melbourne. Professor's personal secretary Ceil became a very dear friend of the family and later became Godmother to my son. She was an incredible human being, kind to patients and relatives alike, and made all the appointments and kept tab on the Professor. On certain days, the Professor would see private cases referred to him by other Ophthalmologists and Ceil got into the habit of making me work up these cases before the Professor saw them. In the days before Auto Refractors, I was known for my good refractions and the Professor soon found this out and I did all the refraction before he saw the patients, much to his relief. Dr Jim Cairns was the other retinal consultant. Dr Hector MacLean was a general ophthalmologist and Dr Peter Henderson the oculoplastic surgeon. On my first day, I was taken to the retinal outpatient of Prof Crock. There was also another international fellow who joined with me, Dr John Chapman Smith from New Zealand. The two of us occupied the tiny cubicles on either side of the room occupied by Prof Crock and we worked cases, which were then documented in the file, and then the Professor would come into either of these rooms, see the patient, and have a small discussion and then tell us how the patient should be managed. The first day after the OP, Prof Crock confiscated the direct Keeler ophthalmoscope that I owned and sent me to go and buy an indirect spectacle ophthalmoscope and informed the dealer that I would pay the money later. That evening,, the indirect was delivered to me, which opened up an entirely new world of viewing the retinal. Over the next few weeks, I became very versatile and comfortable in making retinal drawing; after the first month, I had to work up all cases that were admitted for retinal surgery. At that time, there were very few retinal surgeons in Australia and almost all such cases were referred to the Melbourne unit and so we had a large string of patients waiting to have retinal surgery. I ended up drawing eight to ten retinas every day and assisting in a majority of those cases. John, the other fellow, had taken up anterior segment surgery and so did not get involved much in retinal work. I also got to learn fluorescein angiography mostly from the very experienced and dedicated ophthalmic photographer called John. As per the law, my job was to inject the dye and stay with the patient till the procedure was over; we did some six to eight angios every morning. John became a good friend of mine, and then used to allow me to handle the camera and take photographs while a nurse injected the dye. I remember one patient in particular who was a strapping six-footer, a Merchant Seaman by profession, who would come for angios, and every time he saw the needle, he would faint and fall off the stool. We were caught totally unaware the first and second time, but after that, we would let him faint with the nurse holding on to him, and while he was unconscious, put the needle in and cover the whole area with bandage. We also had one of the earliest models of the Coherent's Blue Green Argon Laser, which was used for treating mainly diabetic retinopathy. Fortunately for me, at that time, the Professor was having some cervical spondylosis and was not able to sit at the laser long, and therefore, he taught me how to do the laser and since then I did all the lasers photocoagulations, which meant that I became quite adept and quick at completing these procedures. So much so that other retinal surgeons in the hospital also asked me to do the lasers for them.

Life at Melbourne was very exciting and yet challenging. A few weeks after staying, the Professor suggested that I buy a car, since I had to take Giri soon for regular checkup, and would need to have a car as she had to be taken to the hospital for the delivery. We had been referred to an extremely nice male gynecologist, who was doing the prenatal checkup for my wife. Since I was in Australia for only a short time and had taken a medical insurance, close to the delivery of the baby, I had to give proof that I had indeed arrived in Australia only recently. And so, I asked some friends how I would go about buying a second-hand car and was told that it was advisable to first join the Royal Australian Automobile Club of Victoria (RACV) and that whenever I found a car to my liking and my budget, I could inform and request the RACV to have the car checked out. I decided one day during a lunch break, in an attempt to buy a car, I walked down to a used car dealer near the hospital and found an old battered *Renault,* which I liked and promptly asked the RACV to have it checked out. It turned out that the car cost only eight hundred dollars, but yet, I needed a bank loan to get this, and once again I went back to Mr Landerman. He rang up the hospital's bank and asked me to go and see the manager the next afternoon. I walked into the bank while the manager was having lunch and when I said I would come back, he said that he could always finish his lunch later and he would be happy to help me (contrary to what we find in most other countries). He said just fill out this form and attach your salary certificate and your appointment order and pick up the check in the evening, of course; I had the invoice given by the car dealer. That evening after work, which had finished early, I picked up the check, went up to the dealer, and in ten minutes drove out with the car. This was a pretty old car but I was still feeling very proud, it being the first car that I owned. I went home, picked up my wife and my daughter, and went for our first drive. Unfortunately, in the middle of town, in the middle of the busiest street, the car stalled and stopped. I had no choice but to ask my nearly full-term wife to get down and push the car, which was fortunately on top of a slope in the road. But she could not even budge the car. Luckily, a few people seeing her plight asked her to get in and pushed it down the slope when I managed to start it. The next day, I changed the battery, and since then, it worked without a fault for two years. When I left after two years. I managed to sell it for nine hundred dollars as well. The car came in handy because we could go visit Mani and Vasu who lived pretty faraway with no other way of reaching them. Of course, it was useful to take my wife for her antenatal checkup and also to rush her to the hospital for delivery. On 24th May, a few days before the scheduled date, my son was born.

My duties also included removing the fascia lata from retinal detachment patients as I had at Manipal, till I showed them that you could store extra without cutting every patient's leg. This soon changed, since I was sent very Monday morning to the city morgue to remove cadaver *fascia lata*. This was cleaned in an Operation Theatre (by me of course) and bottled, gamma irradiated, and stored in the refrigerator, which we used. This went on for nearly a year after which silicon sponge became freely available. Towards the end of my first year as a retina fellow, I was doing public retinas on my own and opened and closed and assisted all private retinas for two or three retinal surgeons.

It was here that I learned the art of man management from Prof Crock. He would never delegate any work to anyone, that he was not willing to do himself (a dictum I follow still). Many cold wintery mornings he would show up at the morgue to help me get the *fascia lata*. This was even more obvious in my second year training in microsurgery; we had some work at 4.30 am on very cold mornings in the monkey house of the university doing some experimental surgery, and he would show up there as well, though he had absolutely no reason to do so. In the winter of 1977, I was posted to Darwin, the capital of the Northern Territory, to relieve an ophthalmologist there who was going on study leave to write his fellowship exam. Darwin was still recovering from the devastation of cyclone "*Tracy*" that stuck them on Christmas day in 1975, and in fact, while we were there, we saw this small sedan on top of the multistory travel lodge building, carried there by the power of nature. Though we stayed there only for two months, it was a wonderful time. We had excellent tropical weather, the Government had given me a brand new sedan to use, and our good friend Ceil managed to get a few weeks off and come and join us there. The Darwin hospital was not busy at all, as they never did much surgery. There was even a backlog for pterygium excision, which I wiped out in the two months I was there. The outpatients consisted of a few refraction and an occasional corneal foreign body cases. The most gruesome injury I have ever seen till then (or even thereafter) was also there. I was called on evening to see a patient they said had been injured in the harbor while unloading stuff. When I saw him, he had this huge crane hook in his left eyeball, impacted in the socket. The eyeball itself was absent. I was not sure if it had pierced the socket and entered the brain. Since there was no neurosurgeon there, we decided to shift him by air ambulance to another major hospital. We later heard that he had indeed survived, but had lost his left eye.

In April of 1977, both John and I had got an extension to stay on for another year. It was during that year, the rudiments of vitrectomy machines started appearing. Professor got into this big time and made his own vitrectomy called VISC or the Vitreous In fusion Suction Cutter, which we soon realized, in our surgery on goat's eyes, had a potential to suck retina in due to the rotation of the blade. The design was quickly changed to an oscillating blade, which would release any trapped tissue when the blade went back and the suction was off.

Once the Professor was invited to a town called Hamilton about a few hundred miles from Melbourne to discuss with an NGO (I think it was a Lions Club) about how to run an eye camp. The Professor promptly told them that he would bring me along since I had already done several camps in India. They had sent a small four-seater aircraft to pick us up and we left early morning one day and reached over Hamilton in about fifty minutes, only to be told by air traffic control about some VIP movement. It was Election Day in Australia, and when we finally landed, we bumped into the Rte Hon Malcom Fraser, the sitting Prime Minister of Australia. Compared to what we are accustomed to in India, he had arrived alone and walked out of the airport carrying his own bag to be received by a handful of people, and off he went to cast his own vote.

I had an opportunity at that time to stay on in Australia, as people in the cabinet were known to the Professor, and he was willing to sponsor me for an Australian citizenship, and he in fact asked me one day to leave our passports with his office and he would see what could be done.

But my dream was not that. My dream was to be back in India and eventually be *somebody* in Indian ophthalmology. I returned to India in April of 1978 to complete my dream of being somebody in ophthalmology in my country.

In April of 1978, we (my small family and I) landed in Madras to be welcomed by the shearing heat of our summer.

Finally in Practice

I returned to India in April of 1978 to complete my dream of being somebody in ophthalmology in my country. I took a bank loan of 76,000 rupees and bought a new Ambassador car for 35,000 rupees and spent the rest to put up a clinic on Poonamalee High Road. I had brought back a slit lamp, an Alcon Cryo, two indirects, lenses and spare bulbs, and several yards of silicon sponge for explant surgery.

A very senior professor of General Surgery in Chennai told me on the day I started my clinic, "It does not matter what you were in Australia or Manipal. You are starting here as zero. So be patient, regular, punctual, honest, and sincere in your work. It will take you seven years to establish yourself." And jokingly added, "If at the end of seven years you haven't, then you are in the wrong place or the wrong profession." It did take me almost seven years from that day to realize and feel relaxed that I was in the right place and the right profession.

My father-in-law had rented out a room on Poonamalee High Road, the then Harley Street of Madras, based on the dimensions that I had sent him from Melbourne. I had visited several friends of mine while in Melbourne, who had ophthalmic clinics and had a fair idea on how to set up a decent consulting room. By the middle of June, I was ready to start, and my father-in-law invited many of his friends and contacts to come for the inauguration. Even before the inauguration, I was hunting for someone to be my receptionist and secretary and found a woman whose only experience in the medical field was distributing medicines in the clinic of a Homeopath. But she was an Anglo-Indian and spoke excellent English and a smattering of Tamil. That's all I wanted. I had never interviewed anyone in my life for a job, so I asked my father-in-law how to go about it. He suggested I ask her to see if she could manage what I expected her to do like collecting money, writing out receipts, answer the phone, and give appointments. Then I asked him what about the salary, and he had a simple formula, ask her what she expects, and give fifty rupees less. She said three hundred, I said two hundred and fifty, and I had a secretary. This girl was running around at the inauguration distributing soft drinks and snacks to the guests when she came to me and said there was a patient waiting for a consultation. Seeing the crowd, the poor fellow must have thought that this was the busiest doctor in town, and was trying to influence my secretary to get an appointment to be seen soon. We gave him also a soft drink and then I took him to my room for the consultation. It appeared he had just arrived by train in Madras and had a foreign body in his eye. It took all of two minutes to remove it and send him on his way, and for good luck that he may bring to my clinic as the first patient, I charged him two rupees. I still remember the fellow's name and his case record, which says, First patient No Charge at any time. However, I never saw him again.

I charged twenty-five rupees as a consultation fee at a time when petrol was selling for twenty-five rupees a gallon (five liters). I was running between three different hospitals in Chennai. I used to travel once a month to Trichy at the invitation of Dr Rajasekar to help Dr Srinivasan and Dr Sathya Albert with their retinal surgery, traveled to Manipal once in two months to help them setup a full-fledged retina service, and on the return stopped for a couple of days at Dr Oommen's clinic in Cannanore to help him with his retinal cases. These were very tiring and exhausting times.

Around that time the video cassette recorder (VCR) and the cheaper video cassette player (VCP, many wouldn't have heard of this) made their appearance and I started visiting a video library near my house to borrow tapes. That is where two significant things happened in my life. Firstly I met John, who continues to be a very dear friend, who worked in that library and started to try and sell the rudiments of an early computer game, called monkey math or something like that. I used to be fascinated listening to his experiences traveling around Madras on his scooter with this game on an audio tape, which had to be connected to a regular TV and loaded. Most people John would say hated the idea of their old black and white TVs even being handled by John. Anyway, that library soon started a computer division, if one could call it that. They had a computer called genie running on basic he was in charge of that division. That was the first time I heard about a computer and John gave me a lecture on the functions and potential. For two days, this concept fascinated me. How nice I thought if I could enter my patient details in that and retrieve it at the push of a button. On the third day I went back to see John and while he was trying to convince me to buy a genie from him, probably to make his first sale, I explained my idea of storing patient details and retrieval. Of course, I had no idea if this was possible and how it would work. Luckily, for me, the second memorable incident happened that day. I was told a very young chap, probably fifteen or sixteen years old was in his office looking for a job as a programmer. John asked me to speak to him and explain what I had in my mind. In an hour-long chat with this young fellow, called Murali, he noted whatever I wanted and told me to meet him the next day. The next day John,

Murali, and I had one fantastic meeting. This boy had drawn a big chart like diagram saying stuff like "If this then that, else the other alternative" By the end of that evening two deals were made linked to each other. If Murali made a program to my satisfaction, I would buy the computer, and if I bought the computer, Murali would get the job. Within one week, both things happened and I computerized my patient records entering the few case sheets I already had in all the free time had in the clinic. I soon realized that if John a graduate in Botany could figure out computers and a young chap like Murali could become a programmer, (the fact that in today's world, my six-year-old grandchild does all this is a different matter) I developed a passion and craze for computers. The next year, at the Kerala State conference of ophthalmology, I presented my program for patient record maintenance and got my first award for the best paper presented at that conference. That kindled in me the thirst for knowledge in this new and upcoming field of science. I had no time to attend computer classes so relied on books. By this time both John and Murali had shifted to another computer company and started selling the Personal Computer (PC). They also sold books. I bought and read these from end to end. I kept updating the PC and my knowledge; I must have read every Dummies book on computer software, when PowerPoint finally arrived, I took to it like a fish to water. Both John and Murali have gone their separate ways and become great in their own ways but continue to be dear friends even now. Murali even going on to develop his own cloud-based hospital and patient management software, making me feel proud that I too had a small role to play in his progress in that direction. John headed several large computer corporations and now runs his own large company into some form of animation.

I tried very hard to get affiliated to a nursing home or hospital where I could do my surgeries and finally a college mate of mine allowed me to operate in his hospital close to my clinic. They had no ophthalmic instruments, so the previous day of the surgery, I had to cart everything there and make a full cataract set, pack it, autoclave it, and leave it in a sealed sterile drum. I did only cataracts at that time and the occasional antiglaucoma. They had a very old anesthetist who was reluctant to give anesthesia since that hospital did not have an ICU in case of an emergency. So all cases were done under local anesthesia, as we did in the camps. I sent many of my diabetic patients for angiography and laser at Manipal so that they were seen by me when I was visiting.

When I returned from Melbourne, I had called on Dr Badrinath one of the most famous retinal surgeons in the whole of India. He was kind enough to give me advice before I left for Australia. He was the one who told me, don't come back with one Indirect and one bulb. Bring spares. So out of courtesy, I had made this visit. We had a nice chat about what I had learned and about lasers, which hadn't arrived in India. One day a few months later, he visited my clinic much to my surprise and pleasure. He wanted to know if I would take care of his retina patients for a few weeks since he was going away to some African country to do some camps (I think with a Lions Group). Of course, I said yes. Two days later, he rang me and said that there was a retina that had just arrived at his clinic and he didn't want to operate him since he would not be there for the follow-up and whether I would manage him. In my heart of heart, I knew he just wanted to know that I knew what I was talking about and my capability to do retinal surgery. That afternoon, I went to his hospital, gave the nurse in the theatre the few retinal surgery instruments that I needed. The next day, I did the surgery. At that time, retinal surgery used diathermy and an implant and required the sclera to be split for the entire length of the implant. Whereas, in Melbourne, I was taught to use the Cryo and an explant, which did not require this. This procedure was therefore very much simpler and quicker than the implant technique. I forgot to say all this to the anesthetist who had put the patient under for a three to four hour surgery, and I finished in forty-five minutes! On the way out of the theatre, I met Dr Badrinath who wanted to know if the case had been cancelled; and when I said that I had indeed finished the case, he was a bit surprised. That probably was one of the reasons he asked me to join Sankara Nethralaya that he founded.

During my first year after returning to India, I was, along with Dr Ananda Kannan, also part of the formative team of Sankara Nethralaya in its first year. There I had the honor, in 1979, of doing the first laser done on a human body in any medical specialty in India.

After that first year, I left that organization and settled down at Vijaya Hospital.

I was invited by Mr Nagi Reddy, the owner, to fill the place left by Dr Badrinath, who was leaving. These were very difficult shoes to fill indeed.

A few weeks after I joined, one day, I was entering the OPD when I saw Dr Cherian standing at the entrance with his hand over the shoulder of a young chap who looked like he was from the armed forces with his handle bar moustache. Dr Cherian said to me" Babu, this is Viswanath. He is my boy ma a good anesthetist. Take care of him."

We shook hands and that started a friendship that lasted thirty-six years. We soon became good family friends and he was and continued to be my anesthetist for all my cases to his last working day. As an anesthetist, he was without doubt, one of the best I have seen. Not only has he anaesthetized my patients, but me and almost every member of my extended family as well.

He was the most well-read and knowledgeable human being that I have ever met. He could freely discuss at great length varying subjects from the Vedas to the writings and teachings in every religion. He was at ease discussing Ancient Indian History or world history to the modern day politics of India and most major countries. I never knew him as a great sportsman, but that did not deter him being informed about every test match and other international cricket matches.

He would rattle off Sufi philosophy with equal ease as discussing old Mukesh songs. He had two passions. His books and his collection of music. He would often say that his requirements were small. He just needed his books and his music and would be able to pass any amount of time. At one time till very recently, he had this obsessive compulsion to read the India Today magazine from cover to cover as soon as it came. He had a photographic memory and could retain what he read for years together.

On several occasions, sometimes between cases in the theatre, he would try to educate me on these philosophical matters, which often ended in disappointment to him because I failed to assimilate what he was trying to convey to me. What one day out of frustration he asked me, "Don't you believe in anything? Do you believe in GOD?" I said, "Yes I do, but I don't believe in religion and its ritualistic traditions". He was pleased with that answer I thought.

I remember a few years ago I had to go to Surat to give an Oration, I had to go by air to Ahmedabad and then was driven to Surat by a young enthusiastic dealer of lasers from whom we had just bought a new laser. There were just the two of us in the car and we were discussing all sorts of things on the way. For some reason he must have thought I was some intelligent chap and suddenly asked me "sir, what is life?" I was taken aback and told him to come to Chennai and I would introduce him to someone who could answer all his questions, (having BVR in mind of course). And the matter was forgotten for a awhile. When we stopped for lunch on the way and were coming out of the restaurant, he said, "Sir, I will come to Chennai, but you tell me what in your opinion life is". I thought for a second a remembered the slogan of the All India Ophthalmological Society, *Thamaso Ma Jothirgamaya, from darkness to light*. So, I interpreted the word life like that and told him "life is the absence of death, like darkness is the absence of light".

He left it at that and was thrilled that I had solved his doubt. On my return the next day in theatre, I explained all this to BVR and he asked me what I had said. I gave him my answer and looked expectantly at BVR for his appreciation. Instead, he had a funny smirk on his face, and all he said was "Stupid!" I did not understand. He said, "So if something is dead it has life is it? "This ashtray is not dead is it? So according to you it is alive." He said quite angrily. I realized my absurdity and told him that I was not smart enough like him so just leave it. A few days later when he had obviously calmed down he sat me down and said, "Babu, you must have some philosophy in life. Don't just go on like this."

I said, "I have, I have!" with great excitement. And when he asked what philosophy I followed I told him the Philosophy of the Lord Buddha "BE GOOD, DO GOOD". He said, "Great, follow that always." Several days later, he gave me a mini lecture in simple terms explaining how that Buddha philosophy was the gist of all religions. Many years later when smartphones came into use, I showed him my lock screen picture with the picture of the Buddha and these words

In 1983, with the help of some well-wishers, I started The Eye Research Foundation, also located at Vijaya Hospital. Later on, my college roommate Ramani's cousin, Jankiraman, who also did MS Ophthalmology in Manipal and whom I was later able to get a fellowship for in Melbourne, also joined me in this venture. We had the first Tunable Dye Laser, which we were told was the first (east of the Suez Canal). I remember the engineer who came to install the dye laser wore a mask and two gloves one on top of the other since he said what he was handling was very toxic. A few days after we had installed it, one day the nurse came and said there was some orange-colored fluid all over the laser room floor. We rushed up and found Rhodamine 6G used in the dye laser leaking from the bottle storing the excess dye the engineer had left behind. It was also about to flow into a large sand bed used as a water filter for the hospital. Knowing its toxicity as the engineer had told, we went into panic. Using several rolls of cotton and cloth using double gloves and masks, we swabbed the place clean and dry. Later that day we called the engineer in London who told us not to panic since Rhodamine was a dye used in Lipstick and that the toxic component was methyl alcohol, which would probably have evaporated anyway.

We were one of the pioneers in starting Excimer laser Refractive surgery, had the first computerized eye department, and developed the first automated angiography reporting system among many other firsts.

It was at that time that I first found a very interesting character in the late Mr Wilson Samuel. He was the pioneer in developing vitrectomy machines in India and a very enterprising individual. Together we worked on many variations of the vitrectomy console. At that time, all instruments for a particular surgery used to be bundled-up together in a cloth and autoclaved. Delicate ophthalmic instruments banged against each other and were damaged very easily. At the time of the surgery, the nurse would remove these and lay them out on the sterile table as required. I designed and Wilson manufactured what I had called the Opsticon (for **O**phthalmic **S**terilizing **T**ray and Instrument **con**tainer). This was an all-in-one tray to store the delicate instruments and they could be sterilized in the same tray where they were already laid out, ready to use.

My first break came when I was awarded the *Joseph Gnanadikam Oration* of Tamil Nadu Ophthalmic Association (TNOA), nearly ten years after starting practice in Chennai (my talk was entitled "Lessons of a decade"). The next year in 1988, at the TNOA conference in Trichy, I was asked to give a talk on *"ophthalmology in the year 2000."* John and I created slides using Basic (PowerPoint was still being developed) and some elementary fonts and animations. I took my Mr. Murali, the PC, the UPS, the uninterrupted power supply, stabilizer, and the CGA projecting device, which had to be placed on an overhead projector (in my car to Trichy. In the dead of night, while all the delegates slept, at Sangam hotel, we set up the equipment and made a place for Murali to hide behind the screen. On making a clicking sound with a ten paisa toy that was sold at temple festivals), he would press the space bar, to change the slide and everything looked so magical. That was *the very first electronic audio–visual presentation* made at any medical conference in India. I did mention to that audience that someday all presentations would be done electronically and that they were watching the beginning of a revolution. Incidentally, TNOA was the first society to stop film-based slides and resorted to exclusive PowerPoint slides many years ago.

Dr J. Agarwal, one of the doyens of ophthalmology in Madras at that time, made me the Organizing Secretary for the 1989 All India Ophthalmological Society (AIOS) conference in Chennai. I didn't know what he based his choice on because he had never seen me organizing anything before nor had I done so. Once this responsibility was given to me, I employed another young fellow called Kannan as my personal secretary at the hospital to help me with my conference work. He was extremely good in short hand typewriting, and so handled all my correspondence and maintained the conference accounts. Computers were just making their appearance then, but between Kannan, Murali, and me, we used it to the maximum in organizing this conference. The PC itself was very rudimentary compared with today's systems, it had a memory of a couple of MBs and the hard disc itself was only 20 MB (which much less than what is available on the Sim card of a modern phone). And yet, we did the entire conference registration on that system and sent ID cards with bar codes to all delegates by post, long before the conference. Bar codes themselves were just making an appearance, and we used these on the card to control people getting into the dining hall. Since the delegates already had their badges, we did not need to sort out the delegate kits name wise, we just read the bar code and gave any bag. This made the work of the registration counter extremely simple. Mind you, all this in 1989. To tempt them to bring this card to the conference, I even offered a trip to Sri Lanka to the winner of the draw of the tear-off tags from these ID cards. The conference itself was shifted out of a five star hotel for the first time. We maintained extremely strict security allowing only entry to people with the ID card. So much so that the President of the AIOS who had gone out of the venue to change for the inauguration was stopped at the gate for want of his ID card. Overall, this was a conference that set a high standard for the many conferences that followed, including the fact that the conference accounts were ready, audited, bound, and given to the organizing committee within one week. Kannan joined as a full-time staff of The Eye Research Foundation. He subsequently did his Masters in Hospital management and Human Resource Management and rose to be the General Manager of this organization.

In an earlier chapter, I had mentioned about a patient called Prabhu whom I came across during my postgraduation days. In the course of my practice (like in every doctor's practice) I have come across some who I can't forget. One of the earliest was this lovely elderly north Indian couple who looked very dignified with flowing silvery hair and a fair complexion, who I had seen in the first few years of my practice. They had been living in Madras for generations and both of them spoke excellent English. The woman had developed cataract in both eyes and needed surgery for both. She underwent uneventful surgery to both eyes with a gap of ten days between the two eyes. After six weeks, she came for her final test and prescription of her glasses. Very satisfied they went away but came back a few days later to get her glasses verified for accuracy. While that was being done she was telling me how they had not gone back to her village for many years due to her failing eyesight and that now she had the confidence to go and whether she could undertake the long journey. "Surely you can," I said. Suddenly she asked, "So I can die now?" Coming after the question about the long journey, I was startled by the question. I said what!!!? You went through this to die now? The husband burst out laughing and said "Doc she wants to dye her hair before going." Whew what a relief.

Another elderly man working in Viswam's office would come to get his eye tested, but every time I saw him, he had the same glasses and never needed a change either. He used to boast that he always wore his glasses even while bathing and sleeping. When I asked him why he slept with his glasses on, and he said he saw his dreams very clearly with them on!

Sometimes patients have the weirdest doubts. I had asked a patient use some drops three times a day and she wanted to know whether to put it before food or after.

One of the biggest challenges to practicing modern day medicine is the advent of 'Google'.

Patients and their relatives, specially those living overseas' seem to think that they know the answers to all medical conditions and make it appear that ten years of medical education (including postgraduation, more if one did super specialization) and forty years of experience can be over shadowed by the click of a mouse. Maybe one day it will happen, but unfortunately, it doesn't work that way, not yet. A few years I had this rustic looking farmer from a neighboring state aged about seventy years who came to see me regarding his failing eyesight. He was brought by an equally old relative of his who been successfully operated by me earlier. The man wore a rather dirty lungi (or Sarong) had another cloth slung over his shoulders. He refused to be seen or worked up by the optometrist nor my residents and insisted on being seen by me directly. His attendant whom I had known for several years pleaded with me to please talk to him and they would follow the required protocol and procedure after that. When I agreed to do that, he came in refused to even sit down and when I asked him what the problem was, from the top of his lungi he removed a rolled up sheet of paper, which he stretched out to me and said "can you give me this?" On looking at the paper, I found it was an email from someone, which read, "To whomsoever it may concern, please give my father Lucentis® injection." This was a very expensive drug injected into the vitreous cavity, often several times, to treat age-related macular degeneration and a few other retinal diseases.

I asked him who this mail was from and he said my son from something that sounded like "buxton". Where? I asked and the attendant explained that he was in Boston. "Is your son a doctor?" I asked. The man had no idea but the attendant said that he was in the information technology (IT) field. I told him that medicine is not practiced that way at least by me. It was not like your son could say, 'give my father a haircut or a shave'. The man took the paper tolled it up and was about to walk out when his attendant calmed him down made him sit down, asked to explain what needed to be done and then explained it to the patient very patiently. Finally after he went through the process I saw him and was shocked to see that the poor man had only a simple cataract. I was angry, very angry and asked the attendant how they contacted this chap in Boston and I was told they have a relative also working in IT in Chennai and he would send some message and the chap in Boston would call this attendant's number. I said "Do that." Within half an hour, he called and the phone was given to me. I did not mince any words telling him what I thought about his 'Google' diagnosis. He kept arguing that he searched for decreased vision in the elderly and found this diagnosis and treatment!! He still didn't think his father needed cataract surgery and nothing more than an injection. I hung up in disgust and told these people to decide what to do. They must have all sat down with friends and family and taken a collective decision to convince the stubborn old man. A few weeks later, they came back with a full entourage and got operated and was more than pleased by the result. Several months later, this 'Boston Googler,' as I referred to him, showed up at my OPD with his father, a bottle of Perfume and a box of chocolates. It was a quiet OP, we had a long chat, and I explained to him the dangers and bad manners of sitting in another continent and making diagnosis and then trying to advice doctors what to do. He apologized profusely for that and said that as children staying far away from their parents they feel obliged to offer all help they can. I told him that in my field of medicine this was not that much of a problem but it was a big nuisance for some doctors. A cardiologist friend of mine called this the "Home Alone Parents" Syndrome, where elderly parents are alone at home, children are overseas and doing well. Father or mother gets a heart attack, children can't come so they have a guilty conscience to do whatever they think they can, including calling the doctor two or three times a day and even suggesting which stent to put and emphasizing that money was no problem. Anyway, I explained to him that his search itself was wrong because age-related macular degeneration was the leading cause of blindness in the western world and that if he had searched for leading cause of blindness in the elderly in India he would have found that cataract ranked above everything else. He left after more apologies and thanks for restoring his dad's eyesight and I never heard from him for a long time. About a year or two later he sent me an email saying he thought his mother needed her uterus to be removed (hysterectomy) since he was convinced she had cancer of the cervix. I sent him a reply with only words "Google Not again." He rang me and changed his request to needing an appointment with a gynecologist!!

On another track, I am reminded of another elderly patient of mine, who I will refer to as Justin, who had been a patient for over twenty years. Over the years, he started losing his hearing until he became stone deaf. But he had this uncanny ability to lip read, which he did with great accuracy. Then he started getting cataracts and the lip reading was not that accurate and he found that very difficult though he could manage a little, specially if people spoke slowly and clearly to him, He came to me at this stage and I found his cataracts needed surgery. The woman who came with him was of no help in trying to communicate with him. I told him slowly and clearly "You have cataracts" and he responded by saying "I have to eat carrots?" I don't know how lip reading works but I gathered Justin picked out the first and last syllables and filled in the rest. I tried again, "You need surgery," and he said "I need to eat carrots on Sunday?" and I gave up. The woman said he had a brother who was good at communication with him by writing on Justin's hand. So, I asked him to come and see me the next day and whatever happened between them but Justin did eventually have surgery under general anesthesia, and he went back to successful lip reading.

Talking of general anesthesia, I myself had general anesthesia in 1990 for a minor surgical procedure given of course by my friend B V Reddy. I remember my roommate telling me that a relative of his had died after a similar surgery and this I had told Giri. So there was great tension in the family and after the successful surgery and after I was shifted to the postop ward, my wife asked our driver to go to a nearby famous temple and do a *pooja*, before I was shifted to the room in the ward. In a custom that I find strange, when a postop patient recovering from general anesthesia reaches the ward the relatives and nurses usually switch off all the lights and draw the curtains to make the room pitch dark.

My driver was a peculiar fellow and often did things beyond what he was asked to do. Instead of doing the *pooja* and bringing back the *prasad*, (sacrament) he got the *pooja* done and brought back the priest as well.

I was in such a room lying on my side coming out of anesthesia, and I could hear a bell ringing, and a light of camphor moving in a circle with a gruff voice reciting some *slokas*. "Oh God," I thought, "I have died and reached heaven!!" Talking of *poojas*, temples, and anesthesia, I am reminded about another patient, a *swamiji* from a neighboring state, who had lost one eye during a cataract surgery done in his state and the disciples who came to see me about fixing an appointment for him said that he was supposed to have lost that eye because he had moved during the surgery, or so they had been told by that doctor. They came to me since I could do this surgery of his other eye under general anesthesia so that there was no chance of the patient moving. I agreed to do the surgery but needed to see the patient first. The patient was brought a few days later and we fixed for the surgery after the required pre-anesthetic checks. I noticed the *swamiji* spoke very few words because one of his disciples did all the talking. The *swamiji* himself was a very dignified looking person with a long flowing white beard and strangely never seemed to use the word "I" Referring to himself, he would always say *swamiji* will get the tests done or *swamiji* will see you with the results tomorrow. On the day before surgery, he got admitted in a deluxe ward room and first thing he did was to get the mattresses and pillows removed. He had brought his own wooden board, which he wanted placed on the floor to lie down; but after much cajoling he agreed to place on the bed instead. When I went for my rounds that evening he was sitting on this board on the bed saying his prayers. He stopped and welcomed me into the room. I told him that next morning he had to be on an empty stomach because of the impending GA. Then said something strange he said, "HE will not eat anything after midnight" I then understood that he does not use the word "I". Either he referred to himself as *swamiji* or "HE" meaning the lord himself. By now, I was thinking that the word "I" should not be used in front of him. So when he suddenly asked me what time the surgery was I told him "HE will operate at noon" He jumped out of his bed came and hugged me and said who is HE? I want you to be operated by nobody else." He went on to live for many more years with good eyesight.

While all these may sound nice and rewarding, and they certainly are, but we need to remember that not all cases have such happy endings. In the hands of the best surgeons, in the best institutions in the world nobody gets hundred percent successful results. I recall two things that I have heard or have been told to me. I once heard sir John Wilson, who himself was blind, who was the President, I think, of the Royal Commonwealth Society for the blind say, "Even if you say that cataract surgery is ninety-nine percent successful, just remember to that one person for whom it was unsuccessful, to him it was hundred percent unsuccessful." I also remember one of my teachers, can't remember who, probably the surgeon Prof Srinivasan, said "If someone tells you that they have no complications, either they haven't done enough surgeries or they are lying." Failures can happen due to no fault of the surgeon, no ophthalmologist in his right mind wants a patient to lose his eyesight; we make every effort to restore it.

But like the literal English translation of a popular vernacular saying goes,

"What what thing Must happen at What what time,
That that thing Will happen at That that time".

As the Wheel Turns—in Rotary

My first exposure to the Rotary wheel was in the year 1968, when my Professor of Medicine, Dr K. P. Ganesan, who was the Rotary Governor in the district covering Mangalore, invited some of us in the third year of medical college to join the youth wing of Rotary called Rotaract. When you are in the third year of a medical college and your Professor of Medicine asks you to join anything, you jolly well join that, even if it is to take classes in Bharatanatyam dancing. Therefore, joining Rotaract was rather a simple requirement. I was made the charter Vice President of the Rotaract club of Mangalore, which was sponsored by the Rotary club of Mangalore. This Rotaract club was probably one of the first ten Rotaract clubs in the world. Because of Rotaract, we were invited to attend Rotary meetings of our sponsor club and I got the occasion to see the Rotary wheel, the Rotary club in action, and hear about the Rotary movement itself.

During my postgraduation in ophthalmology at Manipal, I got to see much more of Rotary at the Rotary club of Udupi-Manipal, since the department was cooperating with Rotary in organizing several eye camps in different parts of north and south Kanara in the state of Karnataka. I used to mingle with the Rotarians of several clubs, which organized these camps on an annual basis throughout the three years of my postgraduation. We often went to many of these camps on more than one occasion and met with the same Rotarians or other local organizing committee members. I was immensely thrilled to see the amount of voluntary work that these people did to enable some persons to regain their eyesight through the camps that we conducted.

It was in one of these camps, where we had screened about 2000 people and picked up about 300 people for cataract surgery, I was posted along with the junior postgraduate to stay back in the camp after the three days of surgery to look after these 300 postoperative cases for the next ten days. On the last day, there was the function to distribute these thick glasses (called aphakic glasses) to those people who had been operated. The function was organized by the Rotary club who were the main sponsors of this camp. The function was on the grounds of the school where we had held the camp and they had put up a small stage where the dignitaries sat, while all the patients sat facing the stage on the ground in front of the stage. The club had invited the Rotary Governor as the chief guest and he along with many other Rotary dignitaries sat on the stage. I was also asked to sit on the stage as well, since I was the resident doctor during those ten days. After all the formalities and speeches by the various people, it was time to distribute the glasses, and due to the large crowd of patients who had to receive the glasses, it was decided that they would form two lines and they would come up close to the stage, and the Governor would distribute glasses to people in one line for the women and the President would distribute glasses to the people in the other line, who were the men, as they moved up in a single file in two rows.

Among these three hundred people were an elderly couple who were husband and wife. The man was terribly undernourished and rather sickly looking was probably about eighty-five years old and his wife was about eighty as well. They were also really looking undernourished. During the past ten days, I had come to understand that this couple had both lost their eyesight *totally* in both eyes for the past forty years. They had bilateral hypernature cataracts and obviously had not seen each other or any of their family members for over three decades or rather close to four decades.

A kink in my brain, I believe, made me tell the volunteers to make sure that this old man and the woman came together in their respective lines to receive the glasses. The process of giving the glasses involved either the Governor or the President lifting a green shade that was above the operated eye and placing the glasses firmly on their face. When this process happened, simultaneously for this elderly man and the woman, the volunteers turned them around, as I had instructed them to, so that the man and the woman faced each other, but now, with some vision due to the surgery and their new glasses. I was standing close to them and I heard what this man was saying is to wife (this withered looking old woman). For the first time after nearly forty years he saw her and then said, "*Neevu thumba chanagi idhey,*" which translated literally as, you look so beautiful. I knew then that the start of my career as an ophthalmologist was being fulfilled. We got back onto the stage and while the official part of the meeting was being wound up with the vote of thanks, et cetera, I sat looking over the crowd of these operated people and right behind them stuck on a post was the Rotary wheel through the spokes of which the setting sun was shining.

It was then that it dawned on me that these two people and the two hundred and ninety odd other people that got their vision back, at this camp, not only because of our surgery or because of the cataract surgical technique itself, but because the first cataract surgery had been already done by the *Sushruta*, the father of modern surgery, five hundred years before Christ. I realized that these people got their vision only because of a few dedicated Rotarians had gone up to the villages around the town, up into the hills, found these people with no vision, brought them down, looked after them, got them operated, and would take them back to their villages. Sitting there that evening looking at that Rotary wheel, I decided that I too would become a Rotarian one day.

In the 1980s, one had to be invited to be a Rotarian. My call came when Mr B Viswanatha Reddi, son of the founder of the hospital where I've worked, invited me in 1981 to join the club that was being newly formed as the sixth club in the city of Madras (now Chennai). On 16 June 1981, on the charter night of the Rotary Club of Madras Southwest, I was inducted as a member of the club. We had a very dynamic and strict charter President called Venkata Raman. He introduced us to Rotary and encouraged us to contribute our might in time, money, and effort, so that the Rotary club of Madras Southwest stood tall in the district. I recall that during the first week, he came and asked me what I could do as an eye doctor as an initial project for the club.

I had just started my practice in Madras and I did not have that many contacts nor the means to do a full-fledged eye camp. So I told him that I would think about it and give him a project the next meeting. Sure enough, at the start of the next meeting, he pulled me aside and asked me what program I had in mind. To be very honest, I had not thought of this at all and didn't even expect that he would remember the request. Suddenly, I thought of starting a spectacle bank. And that is what I told him. I said, "sir, we could start a spectacle bank." He looked at me strangely and said we are a new club, a young club, and so how would we go about doing this. There were already a few Rotaract clubs in the city started by some other clubs and so I told him that we could get the help of these Rotaractors to go to the house of the Rotarians or their friends and collect any unused spectacles that were lying around. He looked rather puzzled and asked me again and then what will you do with them?, and I said that I would check them, make sure that they were not damaged, and then pack them in containers or cases depending on their size and power and label them accordingly. These could then be distributed to people who needed them and that would be a good project. He raised his eyebrows at me and asked me where and how we would store them till they were distributed and how were we going to find people who needed them. I told him that we could inform other Rotary clubs in the city to let us know of people who needed them and they would contact me or the club secretary and get them picked up. At this stage, he walked away from me, went and talked to somebody, came back to me and asked me again, "Just exactly, what is your project, explain it to me once more starting with the name of the project." I told him it was called a spectacle bank. He heaved a sigh of relief, gave me a mighty pat on my back, and burst out laughing, much to the shock of everyone else in the hall. "My goodness Babu," he said, "you meant a spectacle bank? All this time I was thinking you said Testicle Bank!!"

We did eventually start the spectacle bank and this President and I got on famously together after that. In the year 1987, six years after I was inducted into Rotary, I was made the President of my club.

That was the year that Rotary International started their fund collection for the famous Polio Plus program that Rotary launched and eventually eradicated polio from the face of this earth (only the second disease after smallpox to be eradicated from this planet). We had been given a mighty big target by the standard of the economy in those days and yet with the help of my past presidents and fellow members, we managed to achieve this target quite easily. Our club, the Rotary club of Madras Southwest, was also known for a couple of other reasons. We had the highest contribution to Rotary Foundation with all our members becoming Paul Harris Fellows.

We also had 100% attendance in our club on several occasions and were rewarded by the then district Governor. This then became a routine for us and then hundred percent attendance was taken as normal. On one occasion, during a function, when a senior district official visited our club and during the course of the meeting, while we were seated on the stage, this official turned to me and asked me what the secret of our hundred percent attendance was. I should have told him that it had become an habit and that if it was a Saturday afternoon we would all automatically turn up for the Rotary meeting. But instead of doing that, the medical man in me told him that it was a *conditioned reflex*, obviously he had no idea what a conditioned reflex was and he asked me so. Since we seemed to have some time while some report was being read out, I went into details of what a conditioned reflex was. I told him that there was this Russian scientist called *Pavlov* and he had a dog, which had a hole on its abdominal wall due to some injury, and this dog and this experiment came to be known as Pavlov's dog. And what *Pavlov* learned was that whenever he gave meat to the dog, there would be some gastric secretions coming out of that abdominal wound. So, after sometime, what he did in this experiment was to ring a bell first, wait for a few minutes, and then give the meat and the fluid would come out. This went on for a few weeks till the dog got conditioned to the fact that the ringing of the bell meant that meat was to follow, and so after a few weeks, when *Pavlov* rang the bell, the juices would come out expecting the meat to follow suit, this is called a conditioned reflex I told him. So for us if it was Saturday morning, Rotary meeting would follow at noon. He went to the podium to speak and he was congratulating our club for the contributions to the Rotary Foundation and went on to congratulate us for our hundred percent attendance months. And he said, "I asked Babu what the secret of their hundred percent attendance was and he told me that they had this dog..." The audience remained stunned because they had no idea what he was talking about. It was only after he went that I clarified the whole story and then we all had a hearty laugh.

It was customary that the year after one's year as President, some district post would be given by the new incumbent Governor. However, in my case, I did not get such a post. The year after that though, I received a letter saying that the new Governor had asked me to be Governor's Group Representative or GGR (in charge of four to five clubs). I had no idea what this meant, but readily accepted feeling very proud that I had been recognized by the district. One day, I received an invitation to say that the Governor was visiting one of the clubs under me in the city and as the GGR I had been invited. I went for the function and was honored by being given a seat in the front row. "WOW! This is great I thought." The proceeding of the Rotary club went on according to protocol and finally it was time for the Governor to speak. The Master of Ceremonies then announced that the GGR Dr Babu Rajendran would introduce the Governor. I had no idea that I had to do this, as usually the District Secretary had that privilege, nor was I given any material to introduce the Governor with. Embarrassingly, I stood up and walked to the podium and whispered to the Master of Ceremonies that I did not have his biodata. One was promptly given to me by the District Secretary and I proceeded to do the job I was allotted. That day, I decided that whatever role I took up in Rotary or anywhere, I would study my duties thoroughly before accepting the job and then do the utmost to see that I had done justice to the trust reposed in me.

In the year 1992, I got a big break into the office of Rotary district 3230. One day, I got a call from my good friend Viswanatha Reddi. He asked me to go over to his office for a brief meeting. Since his office was just two blocks away, I went there during my lunch break. Viswam, as he was called, was going to take over as the Governor of the Rotary district from 1st July. He wanted to know whether I would be willing to accept the role of this District Secretary. I knew this was a very responsible and very difficult task; but never being one to back away from a challenge and to help my good friend Viswam, I readily accepted. In addition, my dear friend Vaidyanathan was being made Aide to the Governor, so I knew I could rely on him for any help. Over the course of one year, between the three of us and the other office bearers, we managed to make some dramatic changes in the way the district administration was run. The Rotary International President that year was the second Indian to assume that role by Rotarian Rajendra Saboo, and gave a brilliant theme for the year "Look beyond yourself." Incidentally, the present (2015-2016) RI President, Ravindran from Sri Lanka, was a batch mate of Viswam. As the District Secretary. I helped the Governor produce a district directory of all the members in the district administration and members who were office bearers of the ninety-six clubs in the district. For the first time, he also brought out this district directory with photographs of these Rotarians apart from having their contact details. There are two major training events that occur before new Governor takes over. One is the PET seminar or Presidents Elect Training seminar. And for the first time the district organized the seminar outside the city of Madras at a seaside resort where the rooms were occupied by one president from the city of Madras and one from outside the city, thus building a close bondage between the city and noncity presidents. This turned out to be a great success, spread-out over one and a half days. The second training program is called the District Assembly and was meant to train the office bearers of every club; at least ten members from each club were required to be present for this training program, which Viswam had decided would be held at the town called Kumbakonam in the interior of the state of Tamil Nadu.

It was a time when audio–visual presentations were restricted to Kodak carousels. There were no video projectors. We then heard that there was a Frenchman traveling around Tamil Nadu who had a video projector with him, which he was willing to give out on hire, provided he operated it. We got hold of him and decided to project some slides that we had made without PowerPoint, but the problem was that a significant amount of the participants spoke and understood only Tamil, the native language of the state. So, we decided that we would put a running scroll at the bottom of the slides, which gave the translation of the English slides being screened. This of course was long before the concept of scrolling messages appeared at the bottom of TVs, as which is a common feature now. Why I am saying all this is that I was closely linked with a production of the district directory and with the production of the presentation. All staff, the Frenchman, and the projector plus the Kodak carousels were taken with some operators in a van and by road to the venue of the assembly. I was told to pick up copies of the district directory and bring it to the venue by the last train that left Madras for the venue. The rest of my friends, the office bearers, had gone by an earlier train and would make preparations at the site. The night train that I was taking was scheduled to reach on by six am the next morning, so I had plenty of time before the meeting started by nine am. By the time I took delivery of the district directory and reached the station, the train was about to move. Luckily, the first-class compartment in which I was booked in was just at the entrance and I jumped into the carriage, as the train started moving. There were about 200 other Rotarians traveling in that train but they were in the other compartments and were already in the train by the time I reached the platform and nobody saw me get into the train. I got into the two-bedded coupe and found another man sitting in that same coupe. After a brief introduction, he told me he was a medical representative and was going up to a town called Tanjore, and after a while both of us went off to sleep. But before that I requested him to wake me up before he got up got off at Tanjore. Early in the morning, I felt the man calling out to me asking me to get up because he was getting off at Tanjore. So, I got up washed my face and was having a smoke when I asked this man whether we were running late since it was already seven o'clock and he said no, that we were on time. So, I asked him then what time do we reach Kumbakonam? And he said we had passed that station one hour ago.. I said, I was supposed to get off at Kumbakonam, and he asked then, "why did you ask me to wake you up at Tanjore?" For some unknown reason, I had got my geography wrong and thought that Kumbakonam was an hour after Tanjore and not before!! By then, all hell had broken loose at Kumbakonam because Viswam had sent some people to receive me at the station and take me to the hotel so that I could have a quick wash and change before proceeding to the meeting and they did not find me on the train. They asked almost every Rotarians who was on the train and none of them had seen me, so they said that I had not boarded the train. This was before the days of cell phones and there was no way anybody could contact anybody else. There was total panic because I had the district directory I had the presentation and everything would be thrown out of gear by my not being present. So one of them ran up to my wife in Madras and asked why I had not traveled to the meeting and she got very worried because she had dropped me at the station and seen me walking to the train. Not knowing what had happened to me, she called a colleague of mine, and early in the morning, they went back to the station and checked with the station master if there were any passengers left behind, whether any person had taken sick from the station, or any such thing, and they all said that no such event and taken place. By this time, I had reached and gotten off at Tanjore, and the medical representative noticed that I was totally upset and sweating and agitated and he assured me that he would get me a taxi outside the station, which would take me back to Kumbakonam within one hour, by which time I could reach the venue well in time for the meeting. Even to this day, I'm glad that when I finally reached Kumbakonam and walked into the hotel, everybody heaved a sigh of relief rather than giving me a good kick in the back. Needless to say, the meeting and the presentations were a great success and well appreciated. It was a great year that we had, as the Governor kept me busy throughout the year in the administration because of several activities like a multidistrict meeting, when the Rotary International President visited Madras. In 1993, I was made the conference secretary to another district Governor. In those days, it was customary for the Governor to hand over a Memento of some sort to all the Rotarians who attended the district conference and this Governor had managed to get a sponsor, to give a wristwatch with the Rotary emblem on the dial. On several occasions, I was asked to go and meet one of the office bearers of that organization regarding the payment for these watches. On one such occasion, one of the officers asked me in a rather angry manner, why his organization had to pay for watches for Rotarians, and made a comment that he would be very happy when Rotary was not allowed in India. This comment hurt me a great deal and I kept it at the back of my mind wanting to do something at the appropriate time. In 1996, I was made the conference chairman. Before I accepted this post, I told that Governor what happened regarding the watches and I said that I would accept this post only if we did not give any mementos to the Rotarians attending the conference. There was a lot of trepidation as to how this would be taken by the delegates and whether there would be a decrease in the attendees. However, this proved otherwise, and we had a very successful conference. In 1998, I was made the Chairman of the District Awards Committee (a post usually given to a past Governor). We developed a system of points based on the work the clubs did and the whole thing was a very transparent process members; clubs had to submit their reports along with documentation. One of the clubs reported that on World Breastfeeding Day, they distributed 1000 pieces! That seemed rather odd and I wrote back to them saying please send us some pictures of what you distributed! It turned out that they had just distributed some pamphlets on breastfeeding. In spite of holding several important posts in the district covering all activities, my several attempts at trying to become a Governor of the district failed due to unavoidable and still unknown reasons. In 2002, I was asked to be the PET seminar leader for the Governor of that year. Once again, we held it out of the city of Madras in a hill station where Rotarians from the city shared accommodation with those from outside the city. The presentation I had made for that seminar was one of the best I had made till then. We had a great training program and fellowship followed by a wonderful active year.

That training program gave me a great deal of exposure to all the incoming presidents of the following year and I traveled extensively to speak at most of the clubs and outside. This gave me a false sense of hope and I tried for the post of Governor yet again only to meet the same fate.

However, this defeat put me back on the track to concentrate on the ophthalmic societies.

And Some Work for the Societies

People beyond Tamil Nadu heard my name for the first time after that conference of 1989. At that conference, we also won the best video for our movie called *The Worm*. Next year, I stood for election and became a member of the scientific committee of the AIOS; and in 1999, its chairman. As chairman, I found that many awards donated by individuals or organizations had not been awarded for several years much to the disappointment of the donors of these awards. I rationalized all the awards at AIOS and started the ET Selvam award for best poster. I noticed that the very prestigious Rangachari award, which was to be awarded to the best paper at the conference, was actually being awarded to the best paper awarded to a session called by that name. Since this was contrary to the spirit of the award, this was rationalized so that the best paper from each hall got judged again to select the best of the best. This then was the best paper at the conference. At that time, the Chairman of the Scientific Committee had to raise funds to print the abstract book of all the papers. This cost several lakhs of rupees and after doing this for three years, I realized that many company people started avoiding me for fear that I may ask for a sponsorship. I therefore did not stand for a reelection to this post. I made a couple of unsuccessful attempts at being the General Secretary of the society and finally gave up.

In 2003, I took over as the President of the Tamil Nadu Ophthalmic Association. (TNOA). At that time, I discovered to my horror that the TNOA had been deregistered by the government for failure to file mandatory annual reports as required by law. The problem being that the association was started in Trichy and the registered address of the society did not exist anymore. So none of the government notices reached the association office. It was with great difficulty that this got sorted out. In 2004 I handed over the president ship to my good friend Dr Nam at a town called Tirunelveli. Being the sitting President, the organizers of the conference had booked accommodation for me in a brand new hotel. So new in fact that they hung the curtains and fixed the window air conditioner only after I checked into and was sitting in the room. I didn't think they even had their staff in place because I was given a eleven or twelve year old boy to take care of my needs. He continued to sit outside my room as long as I was there. This was in the month of July or August. After a wash and change, I asked this young fellow where the restaurant was and he said it was on the terrace. As I started climbing the stairs to go there, he asked where are you going. I said why when will the restaurant open, he said "It will open before Diwali (a local festival- In November)!!"

He said, now tell me what you want and I will get it from outside and that is what he did for the next three days that I was there. But early next morning, I asked him to get me breakfast and he asked me whether I was an eye doctor who had come for the conference, and when I said, yes, he said "I will suggest something, you go to the conference now, they are conducting some teaching program there for people like you and after that they will give you breakfast also." Little did the poor fellow know I was the President of the same association, but I appreciated his sincerity and the information and knowledge that he had gathered and I rewarded him with a handsome tip when I left.

In 2007, at a conference in Hyderabad, I was elected as Vice President of the AIOS. Out of nearly 6000 members at that time, only about 3000 attended the conference and only some 800 odd came to vote. It was a two-cornered contest and I was declared elected since I got nearly 500 of those 800 votes. The society was progressing fast. We used electronic voting machines (EVM) from the Government of India for the first time and the results were declared within a few minutes of the ballot closing. The 2008 conference held in Bangalore was a different ball game all together. It was an election for all the posts and people had to stand in the queue to vote for three to four hours even though EVMs were used.

I had to do something to see that more people got to vote and never have to stand in queues for so long when that time could be used more profitably by being inside attending a scientific session.

Standing at the podium to deliver my initial address in Jaipur after my installation, even before I uttered the first word, I looked to heaven and thanked God, my parents, and my family, because I knew I had kept my word I had given Prof Crock that I wanted to be somebody in ophthalmology in my country. I knew I had reached that place.

In my term as President, I started the online voting, giving every ratified member the right to vote in the AIOS election without being physically present at the conference. The 2010 AIOS election was 100% online, which no society (not even the Computer Society of India) had achieved. We also released the Endophthalmitis Guidelines, and under Dr Ramamurthy, Chairman, Scientific Committee brought out the much talked about '*Ready Reckoner.*' That year just over one thousand people voted a marginal increase from the eight hundred who voted at my election. However, the election of

2014 saw sixty-seven percent of members who had email ids voted from across the length and breadth of this country and even from across the world. I knew I had left my mark on this society, which is the second largest ophthalmic society in the world.

Finally, a piece of advice for the new generation, "*If you want something done swiftly, securely, safely and surely*—DO IT YOURSELF."

After over two hundred presentations and forty orations/awards (including three Lifetime Achievement awards from Vidharbha, TNOA, and AIOS), I feel immensely proud that much of that work has been original contributions and every single slide in every single presentation has been personally made by me. Nearly four decades of my life were totally dedicated to ophthalmology with sincerity and honesty because it was always an *'I **for an eye.**'*

> *You can achieve anything you want in life,*
> *If you have the courage to dream it,*
> *The intelligence to make a realistic plan,*
> *And the will to see that plan through to the end.*
> – Sidney A. Friedman

Travels and Tribulations

In the course of getting into medical college, during medical training, and more so during my practice of ophthalmology, I have had to travel far and wide on many occasions. Traveling by all modes of transportation, by road, by train, and by air, I have come across some interesting and sometimes amusing situations.

During my hunt to get into medical college, I was finally told that I had to repeat my pre-university exam in order to be eligible. By then, most colleges had already started. Suddenly one day while I was at an uncle's place in a place called Nagercoil, I got a telegram asking me to return to Madras immediately. There were no buses to Madras from there those days. The only train leaving was from a town called Tirunelveli about an hour away by road. I was dropped off at that station just a few minutes before the train's departure. After buying a ticket and entering the platform, I realized that there was no way I could get into the train let alone get a seat, as it was so crowded. Finally, just as the train started moving, I got a foothold on a step and held on to a bar beside the open door. Within a few minutes of the train moving, people seemed to rearrange within the compartment, and I got to sit on the top step with my legs dangling out of the train and occasionally resting on the second step. Just as I got comfortable in that position, I heard a peculiar sound behind me and turning round to see what it was, there in the aisle were three goats!! They were my company for the next few hours; unfortunately, every time the goats passed urine, it would flow in my direction, and I would have to stand till that dried up. Three hours into the journey, the train came to a screeching halt in the middle of nowhere. The train was immediately surrounded by a huge posse of policemen. We came to understand later that there had been a murder in the previous town we had passed and they were looking for the culprit who they thought might have been escaping in that train; I don't know how long we were stuck there but many people got off there in disgust and I found a proper seat till we reached Madras the next morning.

The reason I was asked to return in haste was because a colleague of my father from his army days was the commandant at the fort in Calcutta and he thought he could get me a medical seat if I reached Calcutta in two days.

One day had already gone in the train ride and the only way I could get to Calcutta before the deadline was if I took a flight. We found there was an Indian airlines night flight carrying mail (the Night Mail Service) and got a ticket on that. It was a DC3 Dakota aircraft and I was the only passenger on it. Every seat had a large mailbag strapped to the seat. There was no cabin crew, I think. The flight took off and landed at Nagpur (the physical center of India). Similarly, flights arrived from Delhi, Mumbai, and even Calcutta. While the passengers stood outside on the tarmac, next to the aircraft, the mailbags were repositioned in a different aircraft depending on where they were headed. Finally, Calcutta-bound passengers from all aircrafts got into the aircraft that came from Calcutta and was returning there. I had a few more people for company but I don't recall anybody saying anything to anyone else. We all just slept with more mailbags for company. The flight reached Calcutta as dawn broke and my dad's friend picked me up in his jeep; it is another matter that all that effort proved futile and soon I was on a train back to Madras, to my other uncle's house, which had become my home base.

Another day and another call, and this time my dad's friend had confirmed that I had to do a pre-university course since the A level was not recognized. He also said that if I could reach Ernakulum in Kerala before twelve noon the next day, I would join a pre-university course in a college there. Since it was the last working day of the first term before the Onam holidays, this was my very last chance. Off I went on another train ride. Once again in a crowded unreserved compartment. Those were the days of steam engines; most of which were coal fired; at the end of such a journey, one would usually have blackened clothes and little pieces of coal stuck in the hair and face. That was the condition that I presented myself at 11 am before the college principal. He was aware of my trying to reach by twelve noon, so as soon as met him, he asked me to first pay the fees before the counter closed and the rest of the formalities followed. But I was finally in a college in India hopefully on the way to a medical college.

In 1965, my cousin Ravi and I were called for an entrance test and interview at Manipal. We traveled together with Ravi's father accompanying us from Trivandrum to Mangalore. The instructions with the admit card said that buses plied between Mangalore and Udupi and took about an hour and a half. From Udupi another bus took fifteen minutes to reach Manipal, three miles away. So as we got off at Mangalore; after breakfast, we headed to the bus stand to catch the bus to Udupi. It was pouring cats and dogs as they say, and we heard someone shout out that a direct bus to Udupi was about to leave. Wow, this sounded good! Direct to Manipal, no need to change at Udupi. Three of us jumped into it and soon the bus took off. The roads were terrible and the rain blinding. After one and a half hours when we thought we were nearing Manipal or at least Udupi, the bus pulled into a stand, which had the words *Karkala*. The driver, conductor, and most passengers got off. We asked the only remaining person who seemed to understand English when we would reach Manipal and he said, "Oh you should have gone via Udupi. This is the long way round. This bus will stay here for one hour and then take two and a half hours to reach Manipal." My cousin's father had warned us that we should follow the instructions in the letter sent by the College, but we didn't listen. I can tell you, he was not amused, and throughout the one hour that we were parked there, we were lectured on why we should not be hasty, follow instructions, etc.

We reached late in the afternoon hungry and exhausted. Most rooms available to stay during the test period were gone. Finally, we got one room for three of us that was actually being repaired.

So we got in and felt like doctors. In 1966, when we were in the first MBBS, a group of about ten of us decided to go visit the famous *Mookambiga* temple at Kollur, North of Manipal. We went in two cars and made the two and a half hour journey in just over three hours due to the post monsoon, poor state of the roads. After *darshan* at the temple, all the guys decided to go to the *Souparnika River*. Since it was just after the monsoons, the river was in full flow. After spending several minutes there, many of them jumped in for a swim; about thirty minutes later, we decided it was time to return, but everyone wanted a photograph taken sitting on an overhanging branch of a tree. Since I am no swimmer, I had not ventured into or near the water. I was the only one with a camera and so while everyone got on that branch to pose, I was looking through the viewfinder of my camera and counted only eight people on the branch, plus me that was nine. But we were ten when we arrived! Suddenly I shouted out, "Where is Vaman?" All the good swimmers dived straight back in to the water while a few wandered off looking to see if he had gone to the toilet or something.

A few minutes later, my cousin came up with Vaman in a crunched position all black and blue in color. We got him to the shore and immediately realized he was not breathing. Though we were in medical college, that's about all we could make out. In my school in Sabah, Malaysia, it was mandatory to undergo and pass a First Aid training and certification exam conducted by the Red Cross and I recalled all that training and proceeded to give him CPR after guiding the others what to do. Thankfully, he regained consciousness but remained very agitated and was beating his hands and legs around as if he was having a continuous epileptic fit. We could not accommodate him and four others in the car, so we sent many back by bus and just two of us were with him in the back seat lying across us. We asked the other car to follow, in case this car had a breakdown. We took him straight to the casualty where he was shifted to the ICU. Three days later, the physician called me and said that Vaman's kidney had shut down and he needed urgent dialysis, which was only available at CMC, Vellore. The Dean sent for me and said since I was the college Student's Association President, I was to accompany the vehicle taking him overnight by car to Vellore. A senior registrar and a Theatre Staff (who had previously worked at CMC) were also in the car.

The driver and these two sat in front, Vaman was sedated and stretched out on the back seat and I was on the floor mat between the front and back seats. Every two hours we had to stop the car for the registrar to give some medication and for all of us to stretch our legs. After an uneventful journey of what seemed like forever, we reached CMC and handed him over to the Nephrology department. To everyone's delight, three months later, Vaman was back at college good as new. He continues to be a successful practitioner in Tamil Nadu.

Talking of Tamil Nadu, I recall an incident that occurred while we were staying at the Kaprigudda Hostel in Mangalore. We had a friend, whom we shall call Velu, who got a call from his dad asking him to be present in their house in a town close to Coimbatore for some urgent land registration that had to be completed before some new land ceiling act became effective in the next few days. Velu had an old Fiat car and he decided the fastest way to get there would be to drive. While he was discussing this at lunch, he turned to me and my two roommates Ramani, who was from Coimbatore, and Viji, and suggested we go along for the ride. The young blood in all of us said yes in unison. We left in that car within the next hour and the plan was to drive via Mysore on to the Thimbam Ghats and drive through the Satyamangalam forest to reach Coimbatore where we would get off, while Velu would proceed to his home about another forty kms from Coimbatore. All was going according to schedule, till we were about ten kms from Mysore. Then the fan belt in his car broke and the radiator started boiling over. We were told the nearest workshop was in Mysore and so we struggled onwards stopping every few kilometers to cool the radiator and pour more cold water. By the time we reached Mysore, the workshop was closing and it was only with a lot of cajoling and more money that the mechanic agreed to hunt for a fan belt and fix it. We in the meantime, went off to the famous *Dasaprakash* hotel nearby and had an early dinner. By the time we got the car back, it was past 7 pm and the mechanic warned us that cars were not allowed in the forest road after sunset. We had no option but to proceed to the entrance of the forest and decided that if we were stopped, we would sit in the car for the night and leave as early as soon as the road opened in the morning. Velu walked up to the forest guard at the barrier and spoke to him for a long time and finally came back with a big smile saying that we were allowed to go only because it was a full moon night and the dirt road was visible to some extent. I immediately realized that money had changed hands and the moonlight was just an excuse. Velu had also bluffed to the guard that he was rushing to see his sick or dying father. In any case, we were past the barrier and into the forest. The going was slow, very slow, almost crawling. The guard had said we were to not exceed 15 km/hour, to have our windows up at all times, and never ever for any reason to get out of the car. Velu was older than us and had done this trip through the forest, in the daytime of course, many times before. We three youngsters were beginning to panic wondering if we should have waited till daybreak. To top it all, the guard had told Velu about a lone bull elephant roaming that region and Velu was warned not to cross its path under any circumstance since it was likely to attack and had in fact attacked one of their jeeps recently. The car was getting stuffy. No air conditioning then, windows were up; finally, we decided to lower the widows by a few inches, which made things much more comfortable specially the cool clean air of the forest. We passed heaps of elephant dung along the way, and saw an occasional monkey on the roadside. Oh! We were also told not to use our headlight in the car so as not to disturb the animals and of course the horn was a NO No!. We went along like this for about an hour when we reached the top of a rather steep climb in the gravel road. There was a long gradual descent in the road beyond. Suddenly, Velu jammed the brakes, put his finger to his lips indicating to us to be quiet. In the moonlight that our eyes were now adapted to, we saw a tall dark shape by the roadside about hundred meters ahead of us. Everything was in whispers after that. Velu suggested that we roll up the windows to prevent the human smell drifting out. We didn't know what the fuss was about till Velu said about the lone bull elephant. We waited, thinking the rest of the herd would come and they would cross the road and be on their merry way when we could proceed; but no more elephants came. Ramani thought it was a bad idea that we came at all and suggested we go back to the guardpost till daybreak. We probably would have done that but there was no place to turn around and the closest clearing we could see was closer to the elephant than we were. Neither the elephant nor we had moved an inch the whole night though we kept a close watch to make sure the elephant didn't walk up the path and surprise us. At the first signs of dawn, we decided we had waited enough and began slowly gliding down the slope making as little noise as possible; the plan being to glide down with the engine switched off till we were close to the elephant, then start the engine and race off past the elephant. As we neared the elephant, we were looking for any sign of movement, a head tilted, a turn, a flapping ear, or a swinging trunk, but nothing. So we continued and about 20 meters from what we thought was the elephant stood, an old black and large road roller! We had spent nearly three hours scared of a road roller.

Once I started practicing in Madras, I had to make several trips for professional reasons or to attend and participate in conferences. Two memorable such trips were also by train while I was a visiting consultant to do retinal surgery at a hospital in Trichy, a town close to Chennai. I would often go by the overnight train, reach there early morning, do the surgeries kept for me and then return by an evening flight. This was the routine once a month. On one occasion, I had finished work in Chennai rather late and reached the station and saw the train on platform one as usual ready to leave. As I got in and got settled, I noticed there weren't many people in the train or on the platform as is common when people come to see others off. I sensed something was wrong and asked a porter passing by whether this train was late and he looked at me strangely and said, "This train just arrived sir, where do you want to go," and I said, "Trichy!" He said you better go quick that train is just leaving from platform three! That meant dash across a rather large overbridge, which I must say I managed to just about make it.

Another occasion on the same train same destination, I was well in time and as the train was filing up I lay down and was reading a book. I must have had a very sound sleep. I woke up after several hours and peeped out of the window and could see we were at a station. I didn't bother, since Trichy was the last stop for that train and I would be woken up there even if I overslept. Once again, I woke up after a couple of hours probably close to 2 am and realized we were still at a station. Something didn't seem right so I got off my berth, on to the platform, and realized that we had not even left Madras. Presumably, there was a derailment further up the track and the train had been delayed indefinitely. I quietly made my way back home and later informed Trichy of my inability to come that day.

In the end of 1970, the government of India started a third airline called *Vayodoot* to operate on feeder routes mainly in the North East regions and gradually extended it to South India. The ground handling at these smaller airports was outsourced to private companies, I believe.

These were small aircraft with about seventeen seats (I am not sure of the number but I know there were two rows along the center aisle and one seat in front facing backwards). These were Dornier aircraft and usually flew at a lower altitude. There were two pilots in a cockpit separated from the cabin by a curtain. I had occasion to return to Madras in one of these flights from a town called Coimbatore after attending a conference there.

As I was boarding the flight through the stepladder at the back of the plane, I noticed that its tyres were probably the same size as the Suzuki car I was driving and began to wonder how safe it was. To add to my worries, the person supervising the boarding asked a chap standing there in slippers, holding the steps "*Poria da?*" (translation, Will you go man?). Reluctantly, that fellow agreed. I was the last to board followed by this chap who now carried two thermos flasks and a plastic bag with him. He sat on a jump seat behind me. To his right was the door and in front of him was the door to the toilet. Before we taxied, the copilot moved the curtain and noticed most of the people sitting in the flight were heavily built fat people. He quickly did some rearranging probably to balance the load equally and we took off.

A couple of minutes into the flight when we had levelled off, the guy sitting behind me tapped me on the shoulder and handed me a tray containing plastic cups, some with coffee and others with tea, I presumed. He gave it to me and said to pass it forward. When the tray reached the front of the aircraft, he shouted out saying please give the *driver* also! As the aircraft climbed, I felt as if I was gasping for breath. Was this the end I thought until I looked around and saw I noticed that most of the passengers were breathing with their mouth open. When the curtain shifted a bit I noticed the copilot was wearing an oxygen mask!!.

That airline had a short life due to lack of patronage I believe.

Sometimes, we land in situations most unexpected and definitely uncomfortable.

Once I had traveled to Taiwan to attend another conference.

Taiwan is in a seismically active zone, on so called the *Pacific Ring of Fire*. I for one am very scared of any natural disaster, whether it is floods, cyclone, Tsunami, or earthquakes. As I entered the airport at Taipei, there large signs behind the immigration officer saying that Taiwan was earthquake prone and what to do and what not to do in the event of an earthquake. I was already feeling jittery. When I checked into this posh hotel, not only did they have a similar sign but the reception desk also handed me a pamphlet with the same instructions in various languages. I went to the room and there were these signs in the room and even in the toilet. There were two separate beds in the room and one wall had a wall to wall and floor ceiling glass pane. Lying there on that bed closest to that glass pane, Taipei at night was indeed a very pretty sight. I dozed off to sleep lying there and later suddenly woke up with a start since I heard a nose in the corridor of something being dropped. After that I couldn't go back to sleep and suddenly wondered what would happen if indeed an earthquake did happen, and I realized I was in the bed close to the glass pane and may be tossed out first. Whether it made any difference or not, I then moved to the bed further away from the glass hoping that would give me some additional protection! The next morning while I was in the shower all soaped up, ready to open the tap, the soap slid off the tray and dropped into the tub making a noise and I thought, "Oh God! this is it. This is the quake that I have been warned about." I was wondering what the news items would say back home in India—about a large quake hitting Taipei and the naked body of an Indian visitor all soaped up was discovered!!. Thankfully, nothing like that happened and the next afternoon I was relieved to leave Taiwan for home.

Probably an unexpectedly pleasant experience while traveling was on a return trip from Los Angeles to Singapore by Singapore Airlines. Those days the flights landed at Hawaii to refuel before proceeding to Singapore via Hong Kong. This flight too landed at Hawaii the middle of the night, but seemed to get delayed indefinitely. Several hours later, early in the morning, we were told there was a major technical problem and the flight would not be leaving for a day. We were accommodated in a city hotel. In that group were two senior citizens, a husband and wife, one or both of whom had been operated by me earlier. They were returning to India after a holiday and were accompanied by their relative who worked in L. A. There was also another young girl and then me; we were all the Indians on that flight. The young man arranged to hire a car and we toured the length and breadth of the big island. The first day we had a slight problem with food since all five of us were vegetarians. But the airlines fixed up with a local Indian restaurant and that problem was resolved. We went there for breakfast, lunch, and dinner. The only restriction was that every evening at four all passengers had to assemble at one place for a briefing. We were there for all of three days. What better place to holiday than Hawaii, and that too at someone else's expense? The return flight when we eventually took off had only five of us and a handful of others, the rest having flown out by alternate flights arranged by the airline. The captain even announced that they were carrying the faulty engine back and urged us to look at the fifth engine hanging from the wing.

Once, returning to Chennai from Dubai, by Thai airways, my wife and I were walking towards the boarding gate at Dubai airport when I saw a sign that said medical emergency station and there was a battery car with lights and a few people, probably paramedics standing around. As I walked past, I thought to myself how many emergencies these people would have to handle everyday considering the large volume of people traveling through the airport daily. Anyway, we had just been seated in the business class when there was an announcement asking if there was a doctor on board. I was about to indicate that I was a doctor, when my wife said to wait and see if there was someone one else since I was an eye doctor. But I went ahead and identified myself and stipulated I was an eye doctor. The stewardess said it was okay and to go with her. In the aisle of the economy class, I found a passenger on the floor having epileptic fits and frothing from the mouth. The rest of the passengers were crowding around him and he probably was beginning to choke on his own tongue. I asked the stewardesses to clear the aisle, turned the guy over on his side, and sat with him till the seizures stopped. By then, the same paramedics came on board and were busy attaching an ECG machine and pulse oximeter and recording his BP, etc. I told them to go ahead and do their work but that it was only a case of epilepsy and that he would be fine in sometime. The head of that paramedic team was not convinced since the seizures had stopped by the time they came and saw only this semiconscious, incoherent man on the floor. By then the chief steward had informed the captain, since we were ready for pushback. The copilot was sent out to sort out the issue. If the man had to be offloaded then there would be a significant delay with all the paper work with immigration, offloading the baggage, etc. By the time the man was made to sit in his seat and the paramedics kept asking him his name and to put his tongue out. But the disoriented man did not respond. No one seated next to him knew anything about him. Eventually, they found his passport in his trouser pocket. From his name and address, I realized he was a Tamilian and that he probably did not understand English, which was why he was not responding. So when I asked him his name in Tamil, he gave a name that matched what was on the passport, which seemed to satisfy the paramedic team. I told the copilot it was safe to fly and that he would be fine in the four hours it took to reach Chennai. I told the stewardess to just give him a sip of water and not serve the regular dinner till they checked with me. I had to sign a whole heap of papers both for the paramedics team and the airline and give my visiting card to both of them. Two hours into the flight, the stewardess came and asked me to go see the passenger once more. He was fine and sitting up but said he was feeling hungry. It seemed safe to feed him and told him to eat the food very slowly in small quantities. I returned to my seat and we had an uneventful trip the rest of the way. While standing in the queue at the immigration counter, this chap came and fell at my feet by way of thanking me for preventing him being offloaded (since the passengers beside him had explained what had transpired) as he was returning to attend his sister's wedding the next day in his hometown. He told me this was the second time he had a fit and I advised him to get a neurological opinion and treatment before he returned. Thai airways gave me a bottle of champagne before deplaning with the compliments of the captain, and several weeks later I received a beautiful silk tie from a Senior Thai airways Vice President in Bangkok.

However, probably one of the most different experience on board an aircraft was when my colleague and I were flying on Delta airlines from Delhi to the USA many years ago. We were traveling business class and had had a good dinner and just beginning to doze off when there was an announcement asking if there was a doctor on board. Immediately we identified ourselves and the hostess came and told us that one of their cabin staff was vomiting and if we could have a look at her. My colleague went and talked to the girl and came back and said that she probably had eaten something that upset her. Between the two of us we found antiemetic (to stop nausea and vomiting) tablets and some antacid and gave it to her. An hour later, the hostess said that she was still vomiting and now she had loose motions as well. We were now about three to four hours into the flight and the girl was certainly looking ill. The chief steward then came and told us that another girl also a young airhostess had started vomiting. We realized this was getting dicey and told them that we were only eye doctors and to find out if there was any other physician on board. That announcement was made with no results, and we were it.

The two girls were now at the risk of going into dehydration and electrolyte loss. We asked if they had facilities to start a drip for each of the girls, and they said no. I told the chief cabin in charge that the matter was now serious since we still had several hours flying time to Frankfurt, our scheduled destination. She told the captain and then came back and said the captain wanted to see our passports and some identification about our professional qualifications. Luckily, we had the card issued by the Tamil Nadu Medical Council, which we gave. In a few minutes, the captain came out and discussed the situation. He then pointedly asked us, do you think we have to land and off load them. And we said yes, to which he asked if we would give it in writing, which we also agreed to. They all went off and came back with a bunch of forms and asked us to read and sign. By this time, we were well over the Arabian Peninsula. The captain came on the speaker system and announced about the medical emergency and that we would be landing to off load the girls since their life was at stake. He also mentioned that Delta did not have a presence in most of that region and was waiting for instructions on where he could land. A little later, we felt the aircraft turn sharply, and he announced that we were going to land in Bahrain but the authorities wanted him to dump fuel before landing. He also asked passengers to look out of the window as the fuel was dumped in the early morning sunlight. We eventually landed in Bahrain at about 8 am and were asked to park at a remote bay far away from the terminal. The aircraft was soon surrounded by a ring of armed security men. Someone came on board and took the captain away. A little later, an ambulance arrived and carried the two girls away on stretchers. There was no word from or about the captain for several hours. Some sandwiches and coffee and tea were delivered to the aircraft, which were quickly distributed among all the passengers. We stayed there till early evening when the captain came back and announced that we had permission to leave as soon as the aircraft was refueled. After take-off, he announced that the delay was because the company had to organize for fuel and the method of payment for it. The girls were in the hospital and he told that they were stable.

Las Vegas

In the early 1980s or mid-1980s, the American Academy of Ophthalmology held its conference in Las Vegas. I had gone from India to attend the conference and was staying at a reasonably new hotel called The Dunes. This was one of the newly built high-rise hotels in Vegas at that time.

I was booked one of the top floors of that hotel. I was astounded and taken aback by the size of the lobby in that hotel; it held several dozens of gambling machines and numerous tables, where gambling was going on almost throughout the day and night.

It was also the first time I saw the reception desk was close to the entrance of the hotel and that I had to cross this huge lobby with hundreds of people to get to the lift, which would take me to my room. Our conference was in three or four days, and on the penultimate day there was dinner hosted by the Association of Asian Indians in Ophthalmology in America. I had gone for dinner along with some other friends and returned to my hotel rather high on spirits (both literally and metaphorically). I went up to the reception desk, picked up my key, and took the elevator to the top floor where my room was located.

I entered the room and changed from my suit to the customary sarong (also called a *lungi*). Since I was leaving Las Vegas early next morning, I completed my packing and got into bed wearing only my sarong as is my custom (undergarments). Only after I laid down did I notice a strange smell in the room. Looking around, I realized it was coming from the breakfast trolley, which had been sitting in the room since that morning. I decided to leave it in the corridor so that somebody could clear it overnight.

The room had a rather heavy door with a self-closing mechanism. With great difficulty, I managed to hold the door open with one foot while I pushed the breakfast trolley into the corridor. Before I realized what was happening, the room door *closed shut*!

I tried to open the door but there was no way I could, since the keys were inside the room. That was when panic struck. Here I was, several floors up in this building, locked out of my room, standing in the corridor wearing only a sarong and nothing else. Not even a wrist watch on my hand or slippers on my feet! I looked for a house phone all over the corridor to try and get some help but found none. I had been told that all the rooms in these hotels had very rich people who would have come to enjoy their holiday and have a break gambling and relaxing. Therefore, I dared not knock on another door and ask for help.

After thinking about it, I realized that I had only one option and that was to go down personally to the reception and ask for help to open my door. As crazy as it may sound, I then concluded that (probably because under the influence of alcohol from the party which was still inside of me) that it did not matter in the least if I went down in that state since nobody would recognize me. I was leaving early the next morning anyways and therefore chose the bold decision to "just do it."

I rang for the elevator and it soon arrived and I got in. I noticed that most elevators had a button saying "NONSTOP" and sure enough there was such a button in this elevator. I pressed "L" for lobby and "NONSTOP." The elevator started moving and stopped at the very next floor, where an elderly man and an elderly woman were waiting to get in. He almost put his foot into the elevator when he saw this strange sight of a nearly naked tall Asian standing alone inside. He quickly pulled his foot back and told his wife "We'll take the next one, dear."

And so when the door closed and moved down the elevator kept stopping at various floors. Thankfully, nobody ever entered the lift from any of those floors. Finally, the lift reached the lobby and the doors opened and there I was in my sarong, bare bodied, entering a lobby where hundreds of well-dressed men and women wearing suits and exotic jewelry were busy doing whatever they were doing in that massive gambling hall. While there were other bare bodied people there as well, they were all pretty-looking tall pretty women selling cigarettes and other items!

While I hesitated, for a second, before trying to cross this ocean of humanity, I suddenly remembered what I had thought of just outside my room before I took the elevator down. "What the hell, nobody knows me here, and I will be out of here tomorrow morning anyway," I thought to myself. Then, looking straight forward, I walked to the reception and stood at the counter, which was nearly waist-high. There was a young woman behind the counter doing some work behind her desk. When I said, "Excuse me," she looked up and almost fell off the chair she was sitting on. She could only see me from my waist upwards and didn't even realize that I had a sarong on. She was so dumbstruck that she just kept staring at me not even hearing what I was saying. After a couple of minutes of this, she was out of her daze, and she said, "Yes, sir." I said, "I'm sorry ma'am, I seem to have locked myself out of my room. I need somebody to help me get back in." Without batting an eyelid, the woman said, "Sorry sir, I need to see some form of identification before I can give you a key."

In my inebriated, disoriented state came my reply, "ma'am, all my identification papers are in the room. Whatever I have on me, I'm sure you will not recognize!" But she kept insisting that I had to produce some sort of an identification to get into my room. This went on for a couple of minutes or even more. While I continued to stand there half-naked, she said, "Look around the lobby and see if you recognize somebody who can identify you. That would help." Just then, one of the security people who was also behind the counter, in his own tiny alcove, stepped out and saw me. He recognized me from the previous day's Rotary meeting that I had attended, since he was there, too. As a godsend he said, "I know this doc, I met him yesterday at Rotary. He has come for the eye doctor conference. I will take him up to the room to go and check his ID. I will call you from there." He also gave me his long overcoat to cover with and we went back to the room. While I stood outside the room, he went in and asked me where my passport was (which luckily was lying on the table next to my bed, kept ready for the travel early morning), checked it and called down to the receptionist downstairs and had it cleared by her before letting me into the room.

This certainly must have been the most embarrassing moment of my entire life!

In Conclusion

The only thing worse than being blind is having sight but no vision

– Helen Keller

Vision as far as the eye can see - and beyond

In 1988, I was asked to give a talk on *Ophthalmology in the year 2000.*

In the year 2000, I was asked to give a talk on *Ophthalmology in the year 2020.*

Most of what I had predicted in 2000 had come true and much of what I said for 2020 is fast being achieved.

Hence, I make a Crystal ball look at what

'Ophthalmology may be like in the year 2045.'

Half a Day in an Eye Hospital

In The Distant Future
Dr Babu Rajendran
Year: 2045
Date 12th October
Place: Mega Metropolis of Coimbatore (now including Erode)

Prologue: This is a fictitious situation based on futurologically predicted data presently available. All names are fictitious and any resemblance to any person living, dead, or yet to be born is unintentional. Why 2045? – I would be hundred years old on that date. India is predicted to be the most populous nation in the world in that year at 1.51 Billion. *All images are representative only.*

Time @416[2] Internet time: Narayanan, ninety-five-year-old male, is due for his regular annual ophthalmic checkup. He logs on to his medical website from his wrist bound Evernet connecting device. The screen is projected on to his retina. He does not use any monitor. His eyes control the items he chooses to do. He selects eye checkup. The screen projects the equivalent of today's Snellen's chart and contrast sensitivity screens on to his retina. His responses are recorded. In quick sequence, his optic disc and RNFL is measured and

---

[2] Internet Time is a "new" way to tell time, invented and marketed by the Swiss watch company called *Swatch*®. The current Internet Time is the same all over the World (no time zones or daylight saving time adjustments).

analyzed (IOP is not measured anymore, nor is it found to be important). A rapid retinal scan is done and images captured. Mr Narayanan doesn't wear glasses. Uses just the computer projection device through the center of which he has clear distance and near vision. **(Image 1).**

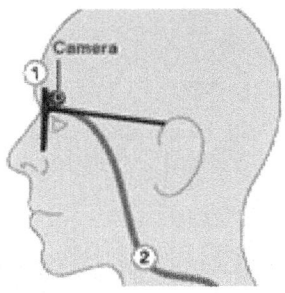

Image 1: Design of projection device used by Mr.Narayanan

Mr Narayanan like everyone else since 2040 has an embedded chip in his arm, which contains his entire personal, medical history including his entire DNA profile. **(Image 2)**

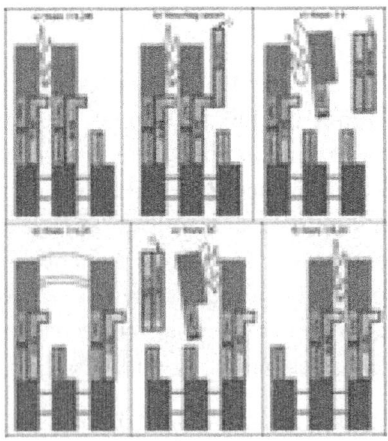

Image 2: DNA profile—Mr Narayanan

He carries no documentation. The chip has all his banking and credit card details, travel document details and identification details as well. After his ophthalmic examination gets over, he transfers the data to the chip. The data are compared to the previous data from last time. Oh! Oh! There is a new change at the macula. His vision is also marginally decreased, his color vision is altered, and Amsler has distorted images at the center. He gets a warning!!! Shall I inform the doctor? He answers. Yes. Then the next question, Dr Sheeba? Yes. A connection is sent out to Dr Sheeba. Narayanan's computer interfaces with Sheeba's computer and decides he needs to be seen. An appointment is made for @916 the same day. The appointment fee and transaction fee are appropriately deducted and credited to Sheeba's account. The whole process took one beat of Internet time (1 minute 26. 4 secs) from the time he decided to check his eyes.

Time: Same time as Narayanan completed his check, Sheeba's computer creates Narayanan's file on her computer. His DNA profile shows he is prone to macular degeneration. His previous history and recent findings are uploaded and requisitions for Mini MRI and DOG Scan (*Digital Ophthalmic Geosynchronous* Scan, unlike the CAT scan and PET scan, this combines anatomical details with functional activity in a single scan) are planned on his arrival.

Time: Sixty beats later, Dr Sheeba sees her **first patient** for the day. Mike Smith, from "Beckam State" (part of ancient UK), has been diagnosed to have diabetes risk recently. His implanted chip **(Image 3)** monitors his various parameters and finds that his diurnal fluctuation exceeded the accepted norms.

Image 3: Implantable chip (enlarged view) of Mike Smith

His DNA profile had told him that he would land up with diabetes and would be warned. His Diabetologist had already seen him and now referred for his ophthalmic work up. Dr Sheeba is an Implantologist having specialized in the implanting of genetically modified material at specific locations in the eye. Mike Smith is about to have his genetic markers removed for modification. The process will take less than hundred beats. She will then implant this material into a tiny nanobot,[3] which she will inject into the two carotids one at a time and then guide them remotely using a joystick and drive it correctly close to the fovea where the nanobot will deliver the genetically modified material, which will then protect his macula from any diabetic-related damage. The process is tremendously costly but Mike's vision is safe for another six years.

Time: Just as Mike is finishing his genetic marker removal, **the next patient** Shankar, who had his eye removed in this hospital[4] following a major traffic accident has come for

---

3   microdevices that travel in our body.
4   Surgery in the true sense, at this hospital is only for Trauma. This was the only surgery they have performed in October. All other surgeries are invasive medical procedures.

his review visit to regain his vision from the empty socket. This is not Dr Sheeba's area of expertise. He has to see the Prosthotologist, Dr Thomas, for that. Today he will only have measurement and scans done for designing and manufacture of custom made socket **(Image 4)** fitted miniaturized camera that will be connected to the occipital lobe where another implant will be placed by Dr Sheeba, which will receive the digital video signal and convert them into microelectronic impulses recognizable to the occipital lobe. The whole procedure will take more than two months. But eventually Shankar will see from his empty socket.

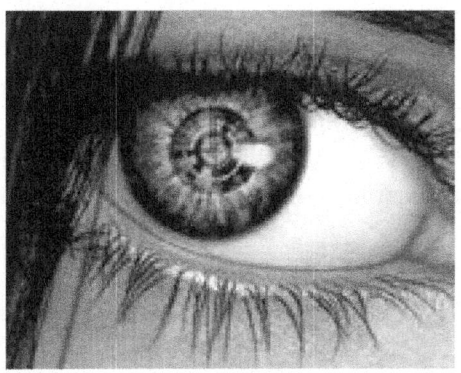

Image 4: Design of the proposed custom made socket for Shankar

Time: **@520** Dr Sheeba's **third case** for the day is a 110-year-old woman, Mrs Lakshmi, who has been diagnosed as a Central Retinal Vein Occlusion in her Right eye. In another hospital, she has already been investigated and the AV crossing identified. Sheeba's job today is to use her cutting Nanobot to reach the site of the AV crossing. These subatomic Nanobots can bore their way out of the artery into the space beneath the sheath and then cut through the sheath and relieve the compression. This is a very highly sophisticated and complex procedure totally under the control of the massive computers recently installed by the hospital (By massive, I meant in power not size, though it is only slightly larger than a present day telephone, it can make trillions of calculations a millisecond). The computer first maps out the entire route the Nanobot will take and Sheeba will simulate Mrs Lakshmi's parameters in it. Her BP, Blood Flow rates, Blood Viscosity, and all the vessel diameters right upto the AV crossing. She will then run a simulation on the computer itself, which will exactly show her where problems can arise, that kink in the Ophthalmic artery she needs to be careful; passing through that, she notes down; when everything is ready, she injects the Nanobot.

The computer has already calibrated its cutters, both the mechanical one (smaller than 100th the size of a human hair) and the ultrahigh frequency Atto Sec Laser cutter. The nanobot and all its components are biodegradable. On a large head-up display in midair she watches the nanobot moving like a tiny submarine towards it target. The going is very slow, as she doesn't want to go up a wrong artery, (she remembers, with sweat building up on her forehead, the one that went up the wrong artery the previous week and how she had to destroy it midway before it got jammed somewhere. She also recalled how she sat watching while the phagocytes had quickly devoured it and flushed it away. The cost in terms of money of that one wrong turn was enormous. She was not going to let that happen today).

She is brought back to reality by the computer alarm warning her in a human voice "***Four beats to target.***" Her hand on the micromanipulator of the robotic controller, her feet controlling the speed with pedals like the accelerator and the brake, she moves closer. "***Locked on Target,***" says the voice. She can clearly see it now. The artery itself is narrowed here due to the constriction of the sheath, though it's the vein that is fully occluded. The sound of the blood rushing past the nanobot is now amplified in the room and as she gets closer to the constriction, the laminar flow changes to a turbulent one and she and the computer have to struggle to hold it in place preventing it from going past the constriction. Double-checking the location, she switches on the mechanical borer and directs it to the wall. In less than a beat, the nanobot is pushed out between the artery and the vein **(Image 5)** and the room becomes silent.

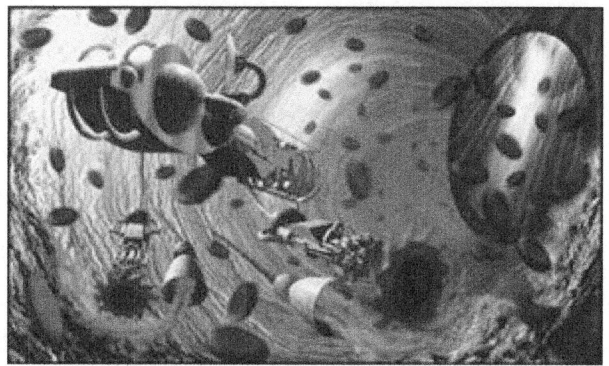

Image 5: Nanobot between artery and vein

She can relax. The nanobot can't go anywhere now. Mrs Lakshmi is wide awake and worried by the sudden silence in the room. Sheeba reassures her and rechecks the position the laser is pointing. The nanobot is turned through ninety degrees and then she fires the laser. There is no reaction (everything is happening at the intracellular level) but the computer measures that the tensile strength of the sheath is decreasing. Suddenly it seems to cut through and the vein and moves further away. A fundus-imaging device looking through the pupil picks up the blood flow in the vein and the computer voice says, ***"Blood flow restored."*** Sheeba still has one last thing to do. Destroy the nanobot so that it can be discarded by the body. With relief written all over her face, she presses the ***"Self Destruct"*** button. As if on cue, the blimp on the head-up display disappears.

Sheeba has finished half a day's work in the hospital. Ophthalmologists do not do refractions or attend to minor ophthalmic ailments in 2045. Each one has specialized in a tiny aspect of medical science combining bioengineering, genetic engineering, Robotics, Nanotechnology, Computer Science, and Electronics. The cost of treatment is enormous, medical tourism is at its peak, and ***even Erode*** is among the leaders in the field of taking ophthalmology.

> *"…to the place where the line between science and science fiction gets blurry"*
>
> – Peter Schwartz
>
> Professional Futurologist

> *"Dreams are answers to questions we haven't yet figured out how to ask."*
>
> – The X-Files

Epilogue

If this little write-up has kindled in you a desire to dream about the future, and what a great time and place it will be to practice your profession in, then I would have achieved my aim of adding this article to the tail end of this book.

Made in the USA
Monee, IL
19 May 2022